NO LONGER PROPE[RTY]
SEATTLE PUBLIC LI[BRARY]

NORTHGATE LIBRARY

APR -- 2019

D0535060

HEY THERE, EARTH DWELLER!

Greenland

Canada

North
America

Chicago   New York

Death Valley   Antelope Canyon

Grand Canyon

Atlantic
Ocean

Pacific
Ocean

Haiti

Mexico

Venezuela

Suriname

Armero

Peru

South
America

Andes

Aconcagua

Argentinia

Spitsbergen

Arctic Ocean

Nova Zembla

North Cape

Iceland
Eyjafjallajökull

Russia

Europe

Asia

Greenwich

China

Alps

South Korea

Sendai
Tokyo

Vesuvius

Pacific Ocean

Iran

Himalayas Mount Everest

Algeria Nile

Ganges Bangladesh

Sahara White Desert

India Mekong

Mariana Trench

Timbuktu

Niger

Vietnam

Chad

Lake Chad

Philippines

Africa Kenya

Maldives

Indonesia

Congo

Krakatoa

Tuvalu
Polynesia

Madagascar

Australia

Cape of Good Hope

Sydney

Indian Ocean

Tasmania

New Zealand

Hey There, Earth Dweller!

Dive Into This World We Call Earth

by MARC ter HORST

Illustrated by Wendy Panders

Translated by Laura Watkinson

ALADDIN

New York London Toronto Sydney New Delhi

BEYOND WORDS

Hillsboro, Oregon

ALADDIN
An imprint of Simon & Schuster
Children's Publishing Division
1230 Avenue of the Americas
New York, NY 10020

BEYOND WORDS
20827 N.W. Cornell Road, Suite 500
Hillsboro, Oregon 97124-9808
503-531-8700 / 503-531-8773 fax
www.beyondword.com

This Beyond Words/Aladdin edition April 2019
Text copyright © 2014 by Marc ter Horst
Interior illustrations copyright © 2014 by Wendy Panders
English language translation © 2018 by Laura Watkinson
This title was previously published in Dutch as *Hé aardbewoner!* in 2014 in the Netherlands by Uitgeverij J.H. Gottmer.
Cover copyright © 2019 by Beyond Words/Simon & Schuster, Inc.
Cover illustrations copyright © 2019 by Wendy Panders
NASA photographs, page 12 and page 25 (Enceladus)
Okapi illustration by Sara E. Blum, page 113

All rights reserved, including the right of reproduction in whole or in part in any form.

ALADDIN and related logo are registered trademarks of Simon & Schuster, Inc.
Beyond Words is an imprint of Simon & Schuster, Inc. and the Beyond Words logo is a registered trademark of Beyond Words Publishing, Inc.

For information about special discounts for bulk purchases, please contact Simon & Schuster Special Sales at 1-866-506-1949 or business@simonandschuster.com.

The Simon & Schuster Speakers Bureau can bring authors to your live event. For more information or to book an event contact the Simon & Schuster Speakers Bureau at 1-866-248-3049 or visit our website at www.simonspeakers.com.

Managing Editor: Lindsay S. Easterbrooks-Brown
Copyeditor: Kristin Thiel
Interior and cover design: Wendy Panders and Sara E. Blum
The text of this book was set in Avenir.

Manufactured in China 0119 SCP

10 9 8 7 6 5 4 3 2 1

Nederlands
letterenfonds
dutch foundation
for literature

Publication was aided by
a subsidy from the Dutch
Foundation for Literature and
the Mondriaan Foundation.

Library of Congress Cataloging-in-Publication Data

Names: Horst, Marc ter, author. | Panders, Wendy, illustrator.
Title: Hey there, Earth dweller! : dive into this world we call Earth / by
  Marc ter Horst ; illustrated by Wendy Panders.
Other titles: Hé aardbewoner. English
Description: Beyond Words-Aladdin edition. | New York : Aladdin ; Hillsboro,
  Oregon : Beyond Words, 2019. | In English, translated from Dutch. |
  Audience: Age 8–12. | Includes bibliographical references.
Identifiers: LCCN 2018027324 | ISBN 9781582706566 (hardcover)
Subjects: LCSH: Earth (Planet)—Juvenile literature. | Earth
  sciences—Juvenile literature. | Geography—Juvenile literature.
Classification: LCC QB631.4 .H674513 2019 | DDC 550—dc23
LC record available at https://lccn.loc.gov/2018027324

FOR SIMON AND ANIEK

(and their grandmas and grandpas)

Arctic
Ocean

North Cape

Hammerfest

Kola

Iceland

Eyjafjallajökull

Norway

Sweden

North Sea

England

Berlin

Europe

Greenwich

Eifel

France

Puy-de-Dôme

Alps

Mont Blanc

Rome

Naples

Spain

Vesuvius

Pompeii

Atlantic
Ocean

Turkey

Portugal

Cappadocia

Greece

Mediterranean Sea

CONTENTS

HEY THERE, EARTH DWELLER!

Take a look under your feet. What do we have there? You can shake your feet, but you won't get rid of it. You can take off your shoes, but you'll still be stuck to it. Elephants, trucks, ladybugs, oceans . . . all of them are stuck to the Earth. We call it gravity.

Seriously, no matter what you do, you'll be dragging that planet around with you for the rest of your life. It's time you got to know it a little better, don't you think?

For example, did you know that many kitchens have a slice of solidified magma for a countertop? (That's the stuff that is found in a volcano.) Or that sea creatures reached the top of Mount Everest before Sir Edmund Hillary? Or that for people living in the northern hemisphere, during our winter the sun is closer to the Earth than in the summer? Or that the North Sea is full of mammoth bones? Or that climate change is nothing new? That there are caves that people can saunter through quite happily, but dogs will drop dead? That you often have stegosaurus pee in your glass? If you can answer yes to all these questions, then give this book to some other Earth dweller. And if not, read it yourself!

In a CORNER of the UNIVERSE

IT STARTED WiTH
A LUMP

Once upon a time, there was no planet Earth.
Can you imagine that? For billions of years, the
universe got by without our sun: without our planet, without plants,
without animals, and . . . without you. But that all changed around five
billion years ago. What if someone had installed a hidden camera back
then? And what if we could now play the film very, very fast? What
would we see?

Bang! A star explodes. Gas and dust spread through space, like
one big swirling cloud. The particles of dust attract one another, just
like the dust bunnies under your bed. So, more and more lumps form
in the cloud. Small clouds stick together, becoming larger. The biggest
lumps collect the most particles, growing bigger and bigger. In the
middle, a large, hot ball forms: the sun. Around it, a disk of large and
small particles remains—heavier particles closer to the sun and lighter
particles farther away.

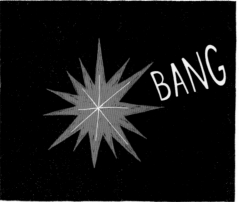

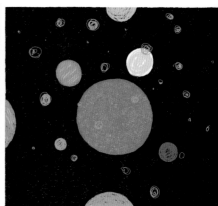

The heavy particles cluster together to make four small, rocky planets: Mercury, Venus, Earth, and Mars. Farther out, four larger planets of gas and ice form: Jupiter, Saturn, Uranus, and Neptune. Leftover blocks of rock go whizzing around all over the place, often colliding with planets. Look, a rock the size of Mars just crashed into Earth! That's probably how our moon was made: the rubble from the collision combined to form a large sphere, which you can see up there in the sky billions of years later.

The young Earth smells like rotten eggs because sulfur vapors rise from a sea of lava. Lots of stones and rocks and boulders are still floating through space. Meteorites come smashing down onto the planet. The energy this releases keeps the surface hot and liquid. But the meteorites also bring ice. This ice melts on the hot Earth, and the water makes the poisonous air thicker. Slowly, the Earth cools down. The liquid surface forms a crust. This crust breaks in various places, and pieces of Earth's crust start floating around.

14

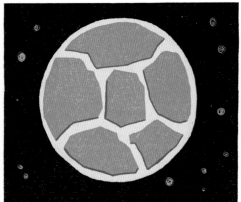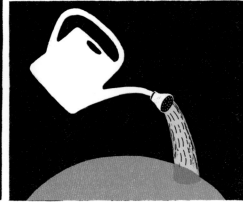

For millions of years, it rains and rains and rains. Then, if we zoom in really close, we can see the first living creatures appear. They live on carbon dioxide (CO_2) and turn it into oxygen, as plants still do today. For millions of years, more and more oxygen enters the air—and less and less CO_2. The air slowly becomes more like the air that we breathe now. It is at the bottom of a layer of gases that surrounds the globe: the atmosphere. You'll soon find out just how important the atmosphere is. One thing it does is make sure that the most harmful rays of the sun don't reach the Earth.

The atmosphere also allows other forms of life to develop, instead of just algae and, later, plants. Life-forms that prefer oxygen to CO_2: animals, in other words. The first animals emerge in the sea. They look a bit like SpongeBob SquarePants, but without the pants and the tie. Meanwhile, the bits of Earth's crust are still just floating around. The first dinosaurs come along, and then the first mammals. Bam! Another chunk of rock hits the Earth. Nearly all the dinosaurs die out, and the mammals seize their chance. Some of them start walking on their hind legs. That's probably your ancestors we're talking about . . .

Earth in a Day

If we squeeze the history of Earth into one day, then perhaps you'll be able to grasp a little better just how old our planet is.

Midnight Earth is born.

12:08 AM	The moon is formed.
3:30 AM	The earliest signs of life appear about now.
5:30 AM	The first algae make oxygen.
9:15 PM	The first fish develop.
10:00 PM	The first animals go onto the land.
10:50 PM	The dinosaurs appear.
11:40 PM	The dinosaurs become extinct.
11:59 PM	The first humanlike creatures develop.
11:59:57 PM	The first modern humans appear in Africa.
11:59:59 PM	Humans spread out all over the world, but not one single human being has thought about agriculture yet, let alone pyramids, steam engines, or the internet.

Mercury 3,032 miles

Mars 4,222 miles

Venus 7,521 miles

Earth 7,926 miles

Neptune 30,778 miles

Uranus 31,763 miles

Saturn 74,898 miles

PLANETS iN PROPORTiON

Sun 864,938 miles[2]

18

Jupiter 88,846 miles[1]

VISITING THE NEIGHBORS

The rest of our solar system formed at around the same time as the Earth. It is a mixed bunch of planets, moons, and other celestial bodies. Some planets look a little like Earth, but there are actually more differences than similarities.

The Earth in Numbers

- The biggest circle around the Earth is nearly 25,000 miles long.[3] This is the equator, which splits the globe into a northern half and a southern half. If you walked exactly around the equator, it would take you almost a year without stopping for any breaks.

- The highest place on Earth is the summit of Mount Everest (29,029 feet),[4] and the deepest place is the bottom of the Mariana Trench (36,037 feet under the water).[5]

- The coldest place on Earth is Antarctica, where a temperature of -136 degrees was once recorded.[6] The hottest place is Death Valley in the United States, at 134 degrees.[7] The average temperature on our planet is around 58.6 degrees.[8]

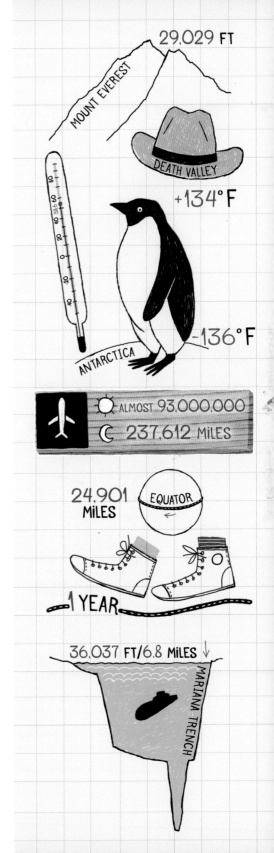

• The Earth whizzes around the sun at about 66,627 miles an hour. It takes about a year to complete the journey. The average distance to the sun is almost 93 million miles.[9] Our moon is only 238,855 miles from the Earth.[10]

Mercury is covered in craters, just like our moon.

Venus has a thick and toxic layer of cloud.

Planet **Earth**: that's where you are now.

Mars is a red-brown color, because of all the rusty iron in the soil.

You can recognize **Jupiter** by its colored bands of cloud.

Saturn is the planet with the beautiful rings.

Uranus lies on its side: the planet doesn't spin, but rolls.

Neptune is the farthest planet and is even bluer than the Earth.

Big and Small

The Earth would fit into Jupiter, the largest planet, about 1,300 times.[11] On Jupiter, a storm has been raging for centuries that, all by itself, is twice as big as Earth. Jupiter, Saturn, Uranus, and Neptune are known as the giant planets. They are farthest from the sun. These four planets do not have a fixed surface, but they do have a small, hard core. They consist mostly of gas and ice. A spaceship would just sink into them.

Even Earth is eighteen times larger than Mercury,[12] the smallest planet. Mercury, Venus, Earth, and Mars are all made up of solid ground. That's why they're known as the terrestrial planets, because the Latin word *terra* means "earth." They are the planets that are closest to the sun.

Light and Heavy

As some planets are much larger, they also have much more gravity. That means that they pull harder on things. So, a cup would fall harder onto the "ground" on Jupiter than on Earth. That's why you'd weigh much more on Jupiter too. Someone who weighs 77 pounds on Earth would weigh 180 pounds on Jupiter, even though he's not even the slightest bit fatter. If you want to improve your personal best in the high jump, you'd be best off going to Mars or Mercury. Someone who weighs 77 pounds would weigh only about 29 pounds there.[13] Walking would be more like floating. Venus is a special case. You'd weigh a bit less than on Earth, but the thick atmosphere makes the air there very heavy. It would feel like being half a mile under water. Unmanned spaceships that landed on Venus were destroyed within a few hours.[14]

Short and Long

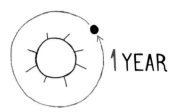

If you lived on Neptune, you wouldn't have a birthday for ages. A year there lasts as long as 165 of our years. That's because Neptune is farthest from the sun, so it takes longest to do a lap around the sun. And we call each lap a year.

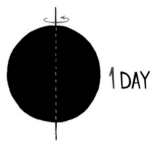

You'd be better off living on Mercury, as a year there is just 88 days. That's Earth days we're talking about, though. Because the days on Mercury itself last about two months: Mercury does a full turn around its axis in 59 days. That would be one exhausting birthday party.

So, how about Venus? A day there lasts longer than a year. Venus turns around the sun in 224 Earth days, but takes 243 Earth days to turn around its axis. So you'd get another year older during your birthday party. That kind of thing is almost impossible for an Earth dweller to grasp.[15]

Warm and Cold

You think a heat wave on Earth is hot? Then you should try Mercury. It can easily get up to above 800 degrees. That's because the planet's so close to the sun, of course. But it really cools down at night, to over 300 degrees below zero, because Mercury has no atmosphere to keep in the warmth. As soon as the sun goes down, all the heat disappears back into space.

Venus does have an atmosphere. And what an atmosphere! It's absolutely packed with gases, mainly carbon dioxide. Add in the clouds of sulfuric acid and you've got a hothouse that even the biggest sauna fan would want to avoid. The atmosphere means that it can get up to 850 degrees on Venus, and it barely cools down at night. After Venus, each planet gets colder, the farther you are from the sun. Neptune is the coldest: it stays at about 320 degrees below zero.[16]

22

Moons and Rocks

And that's just the planets. The moons that revolve around the planets are just as bizarre. Some of them are tiny; others are bigger than Mercury. Some are beautifully round; other are more like lumpy potatoes. Some of them have lakes of sulfur; others have volcanoes full of water. In total, there are more than 170 moons in our solar system.[17]

Between Mars and Jupiter, there's also the asteroid belt, where millions of rocks are floating around. Some of them are just a few feet in diameter and others are as big as mountains. They were left over from the birth of the solar system—lumps that did not merge to form planets and moons.

Finally, if you go past Neptune, you can meet Pluto, a dwarf planet. Pluto is too big for a planetoid, but too small to be called a planet.[18] From Pluto, the sun would look about as big as other stars, although it would be a very bright one. This is still only halfway through the solar system, though. But beyond Pluto, there are just some bits of rock and icy junk floating around.

PLUTO

MY VERY EASY METHOD, JUST STITCH UGLY NIGHTGOWNS

This is a mnemonic to help you remember the order of the planets. Each initial letter stands for the first letter of a planet: Mercury Venus Earth Mars Jupiter Saturn Uranus Neptune. If you want to tell the difference between Mercury and Mars, you can use the first two letters of each of these two planets: **M**en **V**ery **E**asily **M**anage, **J**ust **S**hovel **U**p **N**achos.

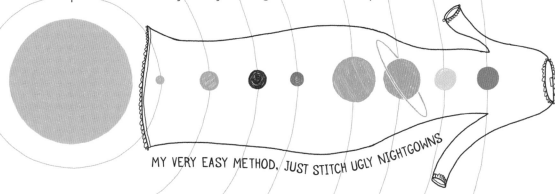

MY VERY EASY METHOD, JUST STITCH UGLY NIGHTGOWNS

Moons

In and around the eight planets in our solar system you'll find more than 170 moons. New ones are still being discovered every year.

VESTA

RHEA

GANYMEDE

IO

DEIMOS

PHOBOS

THE MOON

. . . 168, 169, 170, moons? . . .

TETHYS

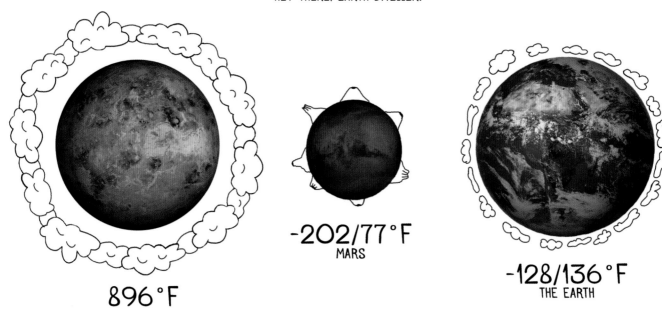

896°F

-202/77°F
MARS

-128/136°F
THE EARTH

SPOT THE DiFFERENCE

There are only two planets that are a little bit like the Earth. They are our neighbors, Venus and Mars. Can you spot the four differences?* If you look closely at the differences, you will see immediately why we live on Earth and not on one of those other planets.

The Biggest Difference

If you could zoom in on Earth, you would discover another important difference. First, you'd see all kinds of satellites orbiting Earth. Inside one of them, you'd see a handful of people; that's ISS, the International Space Station. Lower in the atmosphere, you'd see thousands of airplanes. And maybe a lost eagle or two. Most of the planes would be packed with anxious people with nowhere to put their legs. Then you'd see patches of green across the

Earth. Trees, grass, and other plants. You won't see those on other planets. A little closer to the ground, you'll meet birds and the first flying insects. The lower you come, the more of them you'll see. The planet is teeming with them. Close to the Earth, the bats come to join them. The ground is full of life. A pack of wolves here, a herd of wildebeests there. And there's a crowd of people yelling around a green field. Zoom in even closer, until your nose is almost touching the ground.

Now you'll finally see the smallest creatures. The land is crawling with ants, beetles, lice, and other insects. If you look through a microscope, you'll see the bacteria too. They live to a depth of about half a mile in the ground. Creatures like worms and moles don't go any deeper than a few feet. The layer of life that lies around the Earth really is thin. But take a look in the water. Every little corner is full of life—beasties that are too small to see and fish that are as big as airplanes. Even at a depth of almost seven miles, in the Mariana Trench, you can still find fish and shrimp.[19] So, the biggest difference from other planets is that there is life on planet Earth. And there's plenty of it!

*Answers

1. Venus and Earth are about the same size and weight. That means that gravity is about the same too. If you weigh 77 pounds on Earth, then you'd weigh almost 70 pounds on Venus. But Mars is much smaller and lighter, so you'd weigh only 29 pounds there.

2. Venus has a very dense atmosphere. The air is much heavier. The atmosphere of Mars is very thin. Oxygen is in scarce supply on both planets.

3. The dense atmosphere on Venus means the planet has no chance to cool down. It's nearly always about 900 degrees. On Mars, the temperatures are a bit like ours. They range from about -200 to 75 degrees.

4. Earth has liquid water. There is water on Mars, in the soil and the icecaps, but it's frozen. On Venus, there is not a drop to be found.

Just like Goldilocks

As far as we know, the Earth is the only place in the universe where life can be found. What makes our planet such a great place to live? The most important factor is that the Earth lies within the habitable zone of the sun—at a distance from the sun where it's not too warm and it's not too cold. Astronomers call this the Goldilocks Zone, after the little girl from the fairy tale.[20] You know the one: There are three bears living in a cottage, and they've made three bowls of porridge. They go for a walk to give the porridge time to cool down. Then Goldilocks comes along. She slips into the cottage and sees the bowls on the table. She tries the first bowl, but the porridge is too hot. She tries the second bowl, but the porridge is too cold. Then she tries the third bowl. That porridge is just right. So she eats it all up.

It's the same with planets. For life to exist there, they have to be not too hot *and* not too cold. If the temperature is between 0 and 212 degrees, it might be possible to find liquid water there. And we need liquid water for life as we know it. That means that the planet is in the Goldilocks Zone. Just like Earth.

What happened to Goldilocks in the end? You can look that up for yourselves. But I don't imagine the bears were too happy when they got home, were they?

LONG LIVE THE ATMOSPHERE

Without the Earth's atmosphere, it could rain meteorites on Earth, and you would be burned alive by the sun's rays. Without an atmosphere, life on Earth would not even be possible. Most of the water would evaporate, and there would be no oxygen. The atmosphere is a thin layer of gases, like nitrogen, oxygen, and carbon dioxide (CO_2). This layer gives us air to breathe, protects us from the dangers out in space, and keeps the temperature on Earth relatively pleasant. So . . . let's have three big cheers for the atmosphere!

Hurrah!

Oxygen is one of the treasures of our atmosphere. Just after the Earth was born, there was lots of CO_2 in the atmosphere. That was because of all the volcanic eruptions. No one could have lived in that air. But around a billion years later, the first algae appeared, followed later by the plants.

They photosynthesized, making their own food out of water and CO_2. This process also produced a bit of oxygen. Plants breathe in CO_2 and breathe out oxygen. We do exactly the opposite: we breathe in oxygen and breathe out CO_2. That's pretty handy: we give CO_2 to the plants, and they give us oxygen in return. We owe our life on Earth to the plants and algae; they made sure there was enough oxygen in the atmosphere for us.

Hurrah!

The atmosphere ensures that it doesn't get too warm or too cold on Earth. At night, the atmosphere acts as a kind of comforter for the Earth, keeping it cozy so that the Earth doesn't cool down too much. The heat that has collected on Earth in the daytime can't simply vanish. In the daytime, though, the atmosphere serves as a kind of sunscreen for the Earth. The atmosphere keeps out some of the sun's rays so that it doesn't get unbearably hot.

You can also see how it works in weather forecasts. The clouds are a small part of the atmosphere. They work in more or less the same way. On a cloudy night, it cools down a lot less than if it's clear. The clouds hold on to the Earth's warmth, just as the atmosphere does. In the daytime, the clouds make sure that less heat reaches the Earth, as the sun can't shine through them. So, on a cloudy day, it's usually not as warm as on a day without clouds. In the winter, it works in exactly the opposite way. Then, the clear days are usually the coldest ones.

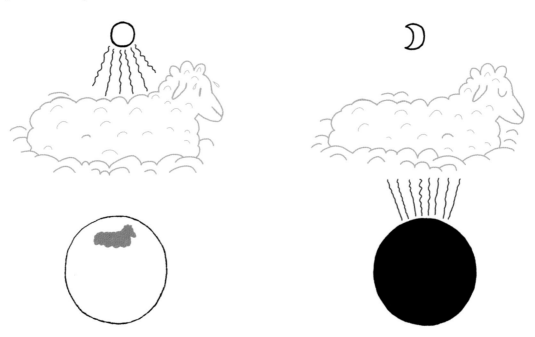

HOLE IN THE ROOF

It's Saturday, April 7, 1990. The Wichmann family from Glanerbrug, the Netherlands, can't believe their eyes when they get home. There's a hole in the roof, and the attic is full of broken roof tiles and small and large chunks of stone. At first they think someone has broken in. But no: the night before, people as far away as Denmark saw a fireball blasting through the sky— and it was apparently on its way to the Wichmanns' place. The meteorite weighed 1.5 pounds when it hit. Before it entered the atmosphere, it would have been about ten times as heavy.[22]

Hurrah!

The atmosphere protects us from rocks and rays. There are many, many rocks flying through space. When they enter the atmosphere, they break up very quickly. This is because they collide with the air particles at great speed. This releases so much heat that you can sometimes see them as "falling stars." A falling star isn't actually a star at all, but a rock or stone burning up in the atmosphere. Usually there's nothing left of the stone. But larger chunks don't break up entirely, as the dinosaurs realized. Sixty-six million years ago, they died out when a giant rock hit the Earth, off the coast of what is now Mexico.[21] Meteorites have also come down in other places on Earth. You can see the craters for yourself on Google Maps. And while you're there, take a look at www .google.com/moon. Then you'll see what our planet would have looked like without an atmosphere.

The surface of the moon is covered with craters. That's because there's nothing to stop meteorites there, and because the lunar landscape doesn't get worn down by water and wind, the way our landscape on Earth does.

The atmosphere is also a kind of shield against rays from space. Ultraviolet rays from the sun, for example. They can give you skin cancer. That's why your parents always come running after you with the bottle of sunscreen every year. In Australia, they slather it all over themselves. Part of the atmosphere is much thinner there than it is in other places, and so there are a lot more people with skin cancer. You see how important the atmosphere is?

THE DOG'S CAVE

Near Naples, Italy, there's a cave called the Grotta del Cane (The Dog's Cave), that's filled with large amounts of CO_2 in the air. People can go in without a problem, but dogs die instantly. Why is that? CO_2 is heavier than air. Dogs are closer to the ground, so they breathe in more CO_2—way too much, in fact![23]

FROM FLAT TO ROUND

So there you are, in your bearskin. You've just gobbled up the last hunk of mammoth meat. You throw a bit more wood onto the fire. And then one of your fellow tribe members asks you: "Hey, what do you think? What shape is the Earth?" So, what do you do? You look around, and you reply: "It's flat, of course. Anyone can see that!"

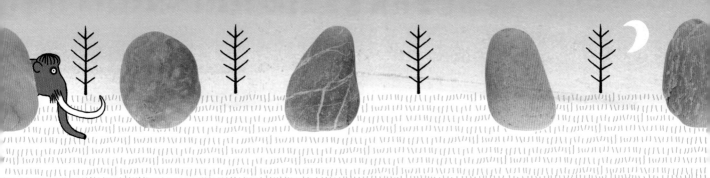

Living on a Disk

It isn't that surprising, really, that
people once used to think the Earth
was flat. That's how it seems when
you look around. Imagine you were
one of the first people wandering
around the planet. And that you had no
internet to look up how things worked. That
there were no pictures of the Earth as a ball orbiting
around the sun. That the whole world around you
looked as flat as a pancake. It wouldn't even occur to
you to start thinking about a round Earth, would it?

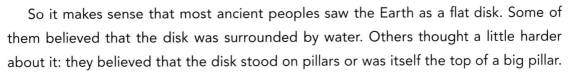

So it makes sense that most ancient peoples saw the Earth as a flat disk. Some of
them believed that the disk was surrounded by water. Others thought a little harder
about it: they believed that the disk stood on pillars or was itself the top of a big pillar.

In Norway, they thought that there was a gigantic pillar or tree standing at the center of the disk. The ancient Chinese thought the Earth was flat and square and that the sky hung over it like an umbrella. There are stranger stories, though . . . From India, for example. About elephants, turtles, or snakes carrying the world. Sometimes even all of them at once: the Earth being carried by six elephants who are standing on the back of a giant turtle who is standing on an enormous snake. That all makes a round Earth sound a lot more believable, doesn't it?

Living on a Sphere

The Greek philosopher Aristotle, 2,300 years ago, found various pieces of evidence to support a round Earth. He saw the hulls of ships disappearing over the horizon while their sails remained visible. Were the ships sinking? No, of course not—they came back the next day. That could only mean that the Earth was round and the ships had disappeared from sight. They had sailed around the curve of the Earth. He also noticed that the shadow of the Earth during a lunar eclipse was always round. So the Earth had to be a sphere, because a flat disk only creates a round shadow when the sun is coming from directly behind. Try it for yourself with a ball and a DVD. Shine a flashlight onto them from different angles. Look at the shadow on the wall. The ball's shadow is always round. The DVD's shadow is round from only one angle and elongated from every other angle. In an eclipse of the moon, the sun is the flashlight, the Earth is the ball, and the moon is the wall. And look: the Earth's shadow on the moon stays round.

34

Nope

Some books and websites make a claim that is not correct. You will read that most people, even 600 years ago, still thought that the Earth was flat. According to those books, Christopher Columbus wanted to prove that the Earth was round and his crew was terrified that they would fall off the planet. But Columbus was simply looking for a faster route to Asia, going west instead of east. In fact, there were hardly any people in Columbus's day who still believed in a flat Earth. His sailors must have been scared of all kinds of things, but not of falling off the Earth.

Okay, So It's a Little Bit Flat

The Earth is not entirely round, though. That's because of centrifugal force. You can also see this force at work when your washing machine is on the spin cycle. You'll see that there's nothing in the middle of the drum, but all the clothes are stuck to the sides. Things that spin around want to get away from the center. You can also see the same thing happening with the chairs of a swing carousel and the dress of a spinning ballerina. The Earth spins too. And the innermost part of the Earth is not completely solid. Just like clothes in a washing machine, even the stuff in the Earth's middle wants to move away from the middle. That's why the Earth is bigger at the equator than at the poles. So the top and bottom of our planet are flat.[24]

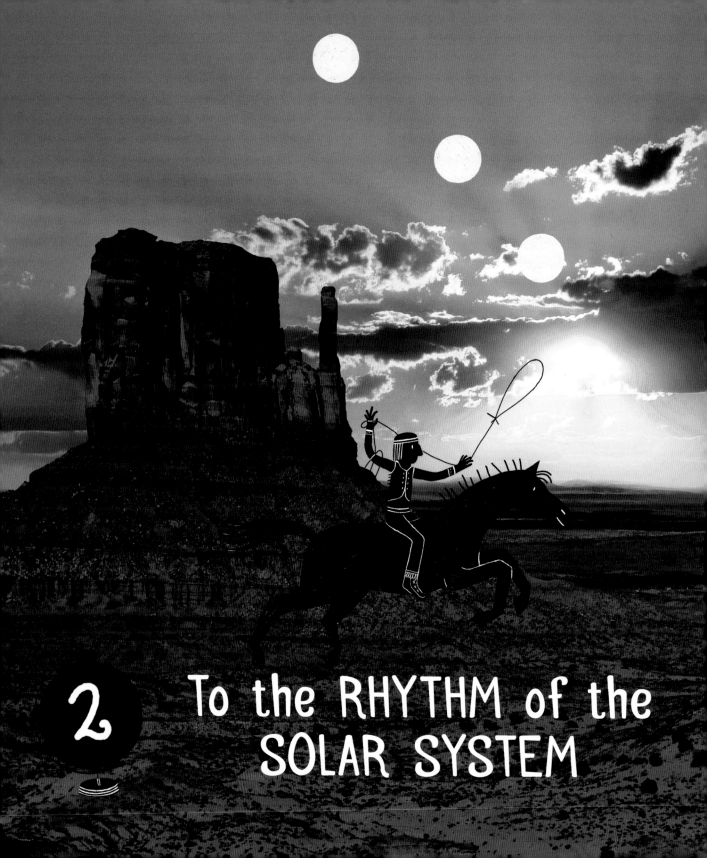

2 To the RHYTHM of the SOLAR SYSTEM

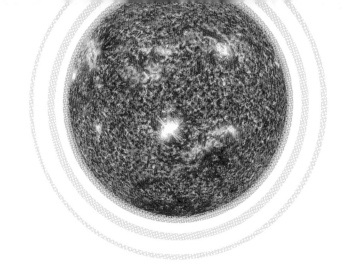

640 MiLES AN HOUR

In the morning, when it becomes light, the world changes. Nocturnal animals look for a place to shelter. Birds start to sing. People come outside. Cars fill the streets. For hours, outside is teeming with life. Until it gets dark, because then everyone goes back inside their houses and holes. The last of the traffic jams disappear and, one by one, people go to bed. Even the most powerful of presidents and the biggest of bullies snuggle up under the covers. They all live their lives to the rhythm of the sun.

Twenty-Four Hours

The rhythm of the sun is actually the rhythm of the Earth. We say, "The sun's going down," or, "The sun's high in the sky." But, in fact, the sun doesn't do much. It's the Earth that spins around its axis. That means that we see the sun coming up, climbing, standing high in the sky, and slowly sinking back down. When we see the sun coming up over the horizon again the next day, we know that we've completed another full turn. Then it's twenty-four hours later. Because a day is nothing more than the Earth doing one spin around its own axis.

The Shadow of the Earth

When the sun goes down, it has simply disappeared over the horizon. So, the sun is still shining, but not here. Where we are, it's dark—but on the other side of the Earth, it's light. We have only one sun, so there's always exactly one half of the Earth in the sun and one half in the shadow. The night is just the shadow of the Earth. If you shine a flashlight on a ball, one half of it will always remain in the shadow. If the Earth weren't turning, we would be in either eternal day or eternal night.

Faster Than an Airplane

You can clearly see the Earth moving when the sun is just coming up or going down—particularly if there's a tree around or some other recognizable feature. With a little

567 mph

patience, you can watch the tree's movement across the sun. It might seem as if the sun's moving, but it's the Earth turning, and the tree turning with it. Just like it's the train that moves, not the cows and houses that you see racing past. If you watch the sun or moon going down, you will also see how fast the Earth actually turns. To be precise, 733 miles an hour. It's true—at this moment you're spinning around faster than a plane flies! At least, you are if you're in parts of the northern United States. At the equator, people turn even faster: 1,037 miles an hour. Why do you spin faster there? The equator is a bigger circle than the circles that run through the United States.[1] So, a place on the equator has to travel a longer distance in the same time, and therefore it has to spin faster. Someone who is standing right at the North Pole or the South Pole will turn more slowly than the

242 mph

little hand on a clock. You can see the same phenomenon if you look at your bike wheels. Spin your bike wheel: the air valve spins around much faster than the axis of your wheel.

As the World Turns

1,035 mph

The Earth spins toward the east. You can see that from the sun and the other celestial bodies that rise in the east. They're not moving, though—it's you who's moving! But why does the Earth turn? It started turning once, and now it just can't stop. The Earth developed out of a rotating disk of dust, stones, and gas. Stones and rocks and boulders of various sizes kept crashing into it, giving the Earth an extra push. That's what gave the Earth the spin it still has.

If you roll a ball, it'll stop by itself because it bumps into all sorts of air particles and because the ground slows it down. But in space there are simply too few air particles to slow the Earth down much. So the world just keeps on turning.

EVERYTHING REVOLVES AROUND THE SUN

The Earth turns, so it seems as if the sun is spinning around us. That's what people actually used to think. Even now, you'll sometimes see a news piece with a headline like "Twenty-five percent of Americans think the sun goes around the Earth."[2] Those people can't have been paying attention at school. Way back in 1610, the Italian astronomer Galileo Galilei said that the sun was the center of the solar system. His Polish fellow astronomer Copernicus had previously written a book on the subject, but he had been unable to prove it. Galilei was one of the first people who was able to make use of a new invention: the telescope. He used it to look at the craters on the moon, the

I spy with my little eye . . .

GALILEO GALILEI

1564-1642

39

rings of Saturn, and the moons of Jupiter. And he also saw that Venus, like the moon, had different "phases": this means that Venus looks different at some times than at others. That could only mean that the planets revolve around the sun. So Copernicus had been right! That was pretty shocking news in an age when almost everyone thought everything revolved around the Earth. The Catholic Church actually said that Galileo had to take back his words. It was not until 1992 that the Pope finally admitted Galileo had actually been right.

ALL THE TIME IN THE WORLD

In some places on Earth, you can jump back and forth between Tuesday and Wednesday. In the United States, for instance, there are eight different time zones. When it's eleven o'clock in Chicago, it's twelve in New York. If you stand exactly on the line between the two time zones at midnight, you can jump to and fro between two days. At New Year's, you can even jump between two years.

Solar Time

But why are there so many different times in some countries? Countries like Russia and the United States are very big. When the sun has gone down in the east of the country, it's still high in the sky in the west. It would be pretty strange if it were twelve o'clock at the same time in both places. Besides, since ancient times, humans have been used to linking the time on the clock to the position of the sun in the sky. When the sun was at its highest point, that meant it was twelve midday. That could be a few minutes later in a place fifty miles away.

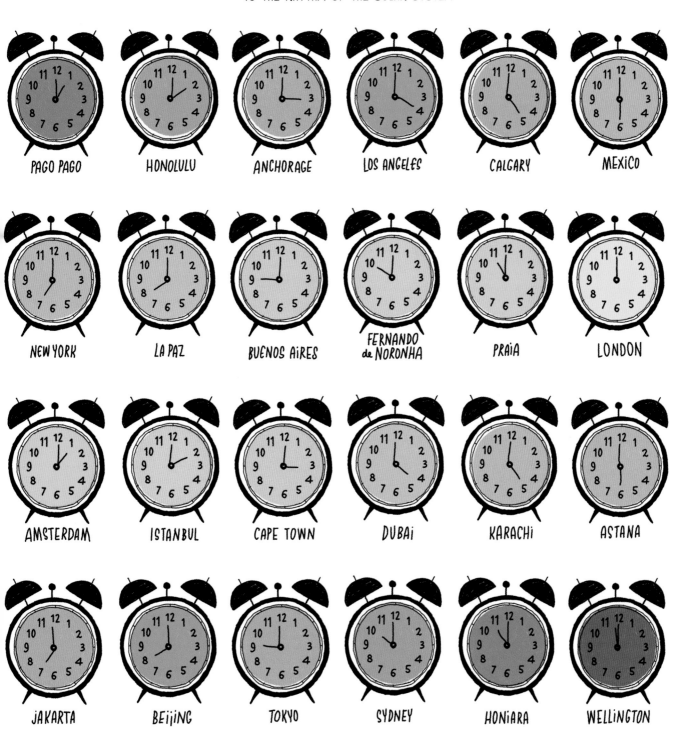

PAGO PAGO

HONOLULU

ANCHORAGE

LOS ANGELES

CALGARY

MEXICO

NEW YORK

LA PAZ

BUENOS AIRES

FERNANDO de NORONHA

PRAIA

LONDON

AMSTERDAM

ISTANBUL

CAPE TOWN

DUBAI

KARACHI

ASTANA

JAKARTA

BEIJING

TOKYO

SYDNEY

HONIARA

WELLINGTON

No Watches

Your grandma's grandma didn't have a cell phone. She probably didn't even have a watch. In the past, people used to look at sundials and church clocks when they wanted to know the time. There were no tall buildings to stand in the way of church towers, so there was nearly always a church clock to look at. People who lived in the same neighborhood looked at the same clock. So, for them, that clock was always right. But from town to town, that time might vary by as much as quarter of an hour. That didn't matter: there was no one who needed to catch the train at 12:17 or who wanted to see their favorite TV show at 7:00. And there was no one who wanted to Skype with their cousin in Canada or to play a game with pKang_04 in South Korea. So it really didn't matter what time it was somewhere else.

Synchronize Your Watches

At the end of the nineteenth century, that all changed. More and more railroads came along and more and more railroad stations. For the first time, people were being transported at high speed, an amazing twenty-five miles an hour! They could use the telegraph, a kind of old-fashioned email, to communicate with one another over long distances. So it wasn't very useful if every village had a different time. How would you know what time the train would arrive? And how could you arrange to meet someone who lived one hundred miles away? So, in the United States, for instance, all station clocks were set to the same time in 1883; the 1918 Standard Time Act made the time-zone system, including daylight saving, official across the country.[3] Countries often made agreements together about the time they would use. The basic idea was still that the sun was at its highest point at around

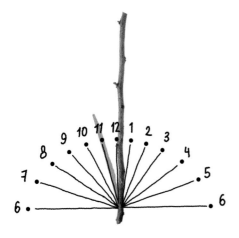

MAKE A SUNDIAL

On a sunny day, stand a pole, at least a foot and a half tall, in an open space in the sun. Notice where the pole's shadow falls every hour. Write the number of the hour in chalk where the shadow hits the ground. So, you'll put a 9 at nine o'clock, a 10 at ten o'clock, and so on. Finished? Good. Then you won't need a clock the next day. The shadow of the pole will tell you what time it is.

Instead of a pole, you can use a stick or a tree that's already there. If you can't write on the ground, then use stones to mark the hours instead.

twelve o'clock. In most countries nowadays, all the clocks tell the same time—except for in big countries like Russia and Canada.

Different Times

When it's three o'clock in Los Angeles, it's four o'clock in Denver and five o'clock in Chicago. That means that you have to change your watch if you fly from one to another. If you fly to Los Angeles from Denver, you put your clock time back an hour. That makes sense: the sun reaches its highest point there an hour later than in Denver. And the sun goes down there about an hour later. That's because you're flying against the rotation of the Earth.

If you fly to Chicago from Denver, though, you put your watch forward an hour. That makes

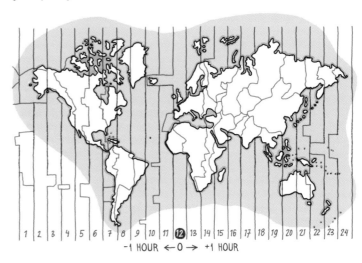

43

sense too: you're flying with the Earth's rotation to a place where the sun goes down earlier. Luckily, you get that hour back when you return to Denver. People who fly to a place where it's much later or earlier sometimes find it tough to get used to the new time. They get jet lag. If you fly from Salt Lake City to London, for example, you lose seven hours of your day. If you fly from Mexico City to Honolulu, then your day suddenly lasts five hours longer. Then your body becomes confused. When should you eat? When you should sleep? That's when you really notice how accustomed your body is to its twenty-four-hour day. You live to the rhythm of the Earth.

HEY THERE, SPACE TRAVELER!

Congratulations on your umpteenth journey around the sun! You are in exactly the same place in the solar system as a year ago. The sun is at exactly the same height. And the same constellations are in the sky as last year. That makes perfect sense, as a year is nothing but one trip around the sun. A trip of over 583 million miles, which you've taken 365 days to do. So now you can figure out how fast we're all whizzing around the sun. That's right, at a speed of over 67,000 miles an hour.[4] That's faster than the fastest rocket that people can build.

Driving for 114 Years

The trip that the Earth makes around the sun is not actually round. The Earth travels around the sun in an ellipse, a kind of egg shape. At the beginning of January, the sun is 3 million miles closer than at the beginning of July. So the sun's distance has nothing to do with summer or winter. On average, our distance from the sun

SUMMER

JOURNEY
OF THE SUN
583
MILLION MILES
108000

FALL

SPRING

WINTER

is around 93 million miles.[5] Imagine you had a racing car that went at 93 miles per hour—that would take you 114 years. But you wouldn't have any time to stop on the way for gas or for an ice cream.

Constellations

In the winter, you see different stars in the sky than in the summer. We only see Orion in the winter, for example. In the summer, it's behind the sun. The astrological sign you have depends on the position of the sun when you were born. The constellation that was behind the sun at that point is your astrological sign for the rest of your life. If that was Capricorn, for instance, then the sun is in the constellation of Capricorn every year on your birthday. It's a bit annoying that you can't check it out. On your birthday your astrological sign is only in the sky during the daytime and not when it's dark. But there are plenty of websites and apps that let you check which constellations are in the sky during the daytime.

Gemini

Synchronize Your Calendars!

It was Julius Caesar and Pope Gregory XIII who came up with the calendar that the world uses as its standard now, which keeps our seasons in step with the months and ensures that the sun is always at its highest on June 20 or 21 and at its lowest on December 20 or 21.

JULIUS CAESAR
JULY 13, 100 BCE

GREGORIUS XIII
JANUARY 7, 1502

The ancient Egyptians had already figured out that the Earth goes around the sun in 365 days. According to them, the Earth made exactly 365 turns around its axis during its journey around the sun. The Roman calendar was based on Egypt's. But then a Roman astronomer calculated that it takes the Earth a little longer than 365 days. Following his advice, Julius Caesar decided that a year would last 365 days and 6 hours. So would you have to add a quarter day to every year? Or to go to bed at six o'clock on December 32? That's not ideal, of course. So Caesar decreed that there would be an extra day once every four years. An ordinary day of twenty-four hours. That way, you could catch up all at once: four multiplied by six hours. The calendar was back to normal.

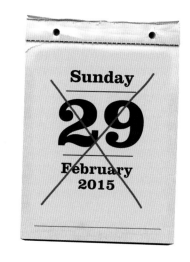

We still use that system. In 2016, 2020, and 2024, for instance, February has twenty-nine days instead of twenty-eight. We call the extra day a leap day.[6]

A Month of Twenty-One Days

But the Romans were not entirely precise about things either. Our trip around the sun is more than eleven minutes shorter than they thought: to be exact, 365 days, 5 hours, 48 minutes, and 45.18 seconds. Sixteen centuries after Julius Caesar, Pope Gregory XIII decided to do something about that. By then, the calendar was already ten days behind. Following the advice of a clever doctor, Gregory solved this problem by skipping

365 DAYS +
5 HOURS +
48 MINUTES [00:48] +
48.18 SECONDS =
1 TRIP AROUND the ● = 1 YEAR

ten days and then scrapping three leap years every 400 years. So people who went to bed on the night of Thursday, October 4, 1582, woke up the next day on Friday, October 15. Too bad for everyone who had a birthday on one of the days in between . . .[7]

Since then, the calendar has been much more accurate, but it is also a lot more complicated. Every year that is divisible by 4 gets a leap day on February 29—for example, 2016 and 2020. But if you can divide the year by 100, then there's no leap day—as in 1900 and 2100. Unless, that is, the year is also divisible by 400, because then we do have a leap day—for example, in 2000 and 2400. That's nice and simple, huh?

THE WONKY EARTH

If you live in the northern hemisphere, in the summer, you run outside in your shorts; in the winter, you stay inside wearing a thick sweater. Meanwhile, on the other side of the Earth, they celebrate Christmas in bikinis and sit by the fire in July. Where do all those differences come from? Seven questions about seasons:

Why Is It Warmer in the Summer than in the Winter?

Ask ten people this question, and half of them will reply that it's because the Earth is closer to the sun then. That isn't true, because in the northern hemisphere's summer, the Earth is actually farther from the sun. Besides, the distance from the sun has nothing to do

with the seasons. Otherwise, how could it be summer in Australia at the moment when it's winter in the United States? No, the reason for the seasons is that the Earth is wonky.

Wonky?

Have you ever noticed the way that globes are at an angle on their stands? You know, those little models of the planet that your teacher or your grandpa have standing around on a shelf somewhere. There's a kind of stick inside them, running from the North Pole to the South Pole. We call it the Earth's axis. That stick doesn't really exist, but the Earth does indeed stand at an angle.

At an Angle? Relative to What?

Good question. The model globe is at an angle to the desk or shelf it's standing on. The Earth is at an angle to the circle it makes around the sun. If you were to draw that whole orbit, you would see a disk. And our equator does not turn parallel to that disk. It has

an angle of 23.5 degrees.[8] That's quite a lot. It's about as far as you can lean back with your upper body when you're standing. So while the Earth is orbiting around the sun, the Earth is at an angle. But the Earth's axis always points the same way. Take a look at the axis in the picture of the seasons.

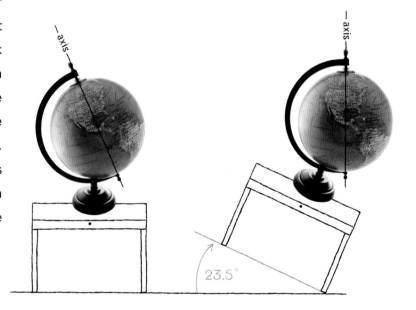

But What Does That Have to Do with the Seasons?

Because the Earth is at an angle, it spends part of the year with its North Pole toward the sun. For people in the northern hemisphere, it gets light early and dark late at that time of year, and the sun is high in the sky in the afternoons. The sun reaches its highest point at the beginning of summer. Half a year later, the Earth stands with its south side toward the sun. Then it gets light late and dark early, and the sun does not rise high in the sky. The sun is at its lowest at the beginning of winter.

And Why Is It Warmer in the Summer than in the Winter?

The sun shines longer, so the Earth has more time to warm up and less time to cool down. Plus, the sun is higher in the sky in summer. You can see that this causes more warmth every day. The warmest part of the day is the afternoon. At around twelve o'clock, the sun is at its highest point and has the most strength. The Earth absorbs a lot of heat then, and we can still feel it in the afternoon. In the morning

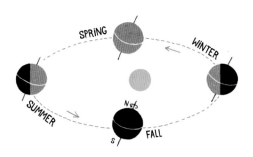

TWO MONTHS OF NIGHT

It is January 21, eleven o'clock in the morning. In Hammerfest, Norway, it has been dark for almost two months. The locals are staring excitedly at the horizon. At four minutes past eleven, the sun will finally come up again. It will go back down again one hour and six minutes later, but the days will now start to become longer and longer. In fact, from May 14, the sun will not set for two and a half months. Sweet dreams!

and the evening, it is usually colder because then the sun is lower and the Earth has already lost some of its warmth.

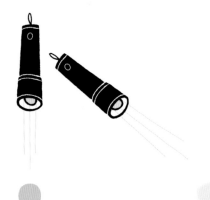

Why Is It Warmer When the Sun Is Higher?

When the sun is higher, more sunlight falls on every part of the Earth and of your skin too. The sun is, shall we say, extra concentrated. Try it for yourself. Aim a flashlight straight at the wall. You should see a clear, round patch of light on the wall. That is how sunlight falls in the summer. Now hold the flashlight at a bit of an angle. The patch of light becomes larger and less sharp. That's how sunlight falls in the winter. There's the same amount of light, but it is distributed over a larger surface. And so the rays of sun can't light up and heat the surface so well.

Yes, but the Days Start Getting Shorter from June 21, Don't They?

You're right about that. The warmest days are usually during the period when the days are already becoming shorter and the sun is getting lower and lower. That's because the Earth is a bit slow. The temperature of the ground,

TWELVE MONTHS OF SUMMER
In Suriname, Kenya, and Indonesia, there are no noticeable changes of seasons. In countries around the equator, the sun is at around the same height in the sky every afternoon. The sun shines for about half the day all year long. The differences in temperature are much smaller there because the sun's rays nearly always fall straight onto the Earth. At sunset, there is only a brief dusk, because the sun dips almost straight down.

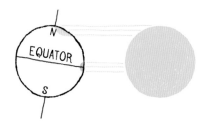

and especially the water, warm up slowly after the winter. That's why it's usually colder on June 21 than July 21, even though the sun is higher in June and shines for longer. For real summer, the Earth and the water have to be all nice and warmed up. In the same way, winter doesn't really begin until January, when the days are already longer and the sun is getting higher and higher. That's because the Earth and the water are at their coldest then.

THE TRUTH ABOUT EBB AND FLOW

Do you want to make your parents stumble and stutter? Then ask them to explain ebb and flow, or low tide and high tide. They probably won't get much further than saying something about the gravity of the moon pulling on the water. Very clever! But then why do high tide and low tide happen twice a day? The moon doesn't pass through the sky twice in one day, does it?

Rescue Your Towel!

Every day, high tide happens twice, and so does low tide. Ebb, or low tide, means that the water retreats, and flow, or high tide, means that the water gets higher. So when it's low tide, you have to walk farther and farther from your towel to reach the sea, and when it's high tide, you might need to save your towel from the rising water.

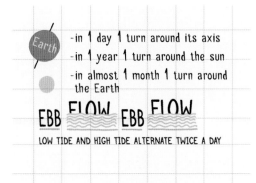

- in 1 day 1 turn around its axis
- in 1 year 1 turn around the sun
- in almost 1 month 1 turn around the Earth

EBB FLOW EBB FLOW

LOW TIDE AND HIGH TIDE ALTERNATE TWICE A DAY

The tides happen because the Earth turns and the moon passes by everywhere on Earth once a day, like the sun. But you don't see the moon every day. That's because it's less noticeable in the daytime, as sometimes it's cloudy and sometimes the moon is on the same side as the sun.

Two Lots of High Tide

The moon revolves around the sun because the gravity of our planet has the moon in its power. But the moon also has its own gravity. So the moon pulls at the Earth a little bit too. And at the water on Earth. How hard the moon pulls depends on the distance.

The water on the side facing the moon experiences the most gravity. So a bulge of water develops. Solid ground experiences a little less attraction, so it pulls toward the moon a little less. The water on the far side from the moon experiences the least gravity from the moon. So it stays farthest from the moon. As a result, a bulge of water develops on that side too. You could just as easily say that the moon is pulling the Earth away from that water.

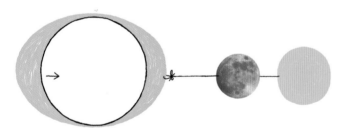

Once More—With Mice!

As it's so complicated, we're going to do it one more time, but with mice. Imagine you have a really big bunch of mice. In the distance, there's a cheese factory. The mice closest to the cheese factory can smell the cheese best and are therefore more attracted to it. So they run fastest toward the cheese. The mice in the middle can't smell the cheese as well, so they feel less attraction. They run a little more slowly. The mice who are at the greatest distance from the factory can smell it least. They head most slowly toward the factory.

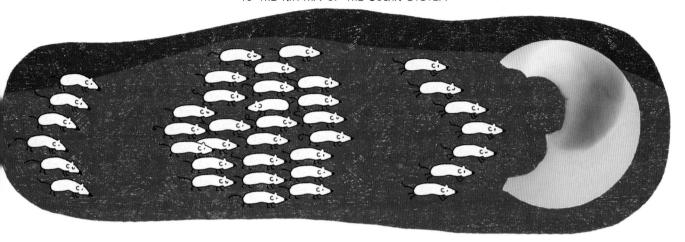

The group in the middle sees its distance from the other two groups growing larger and larger. This is because one group is running faster than they are (they feel more attraction) and because the other group is running more slowly than they are (they feel less attraction). The tides work just like these mice. The group in the middle is solid ground. The other two groups are the mountains of water. And the cheese factory is the moon.

The Strength of the Sun

The sun also pulls at the water. It has much more gravity, because it is so big. But it is also much farther away. That means its influence on the tides is less than that of the moon. But when the sun is on the same side as the moon (new moon), the high tide is even higher. This is known as spring tide. When there is a storm, you have to be extra careful during spring tide, as the water comes even higher. When the sun is on the other side from the moon, it's also spring tide. You can see it as an extra cheese factory for the mice.

TRAVELING FOR DAYS

Tides are more complicated than you think. When the moon is in the sky, it does not always mean that it is high tide. The gravity of the moon mostly affects the largest areas of water—the oceans, in other words. High tide in the North Sea is actually a wave that has been traveling for days from the southern oceans, where there is so much water that low and high tides more or less follow the moon.

On a SEA of BOILING MAGMA

3

About another 2,000 miles to the Earth's core

4,000 MiLES iNTO THE DEPTHS

Let's dig a hole in the Earth. We'll start in the front yard, among the plants. The top layer should be nice and loose. This is a mixture of sand, air, water, and humus (the remains of dead animals and plants). If you dig deeper, you might find clay, peat, sand, or water. The deeper you go, the more solid the ground will be. And after about thirty feet, you'll notice that it's getting warmer too. In the top layer, the heat will rise by about a degree every fifty-five feet.[1] Deep inside the Earth, it's over 9,000 degrees.[2]

The Earth's Crust

The layer you're digging in is the Earth's crust: the top layer of the Earth. It consists mainly of soil and stones. There are plants

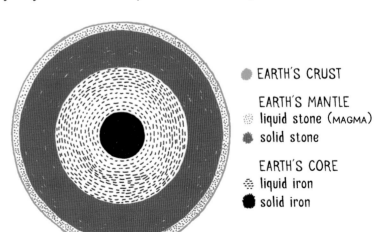

EARTH'S CRUST

EARTH'S MANTLE
liquid stone (MAGMA)
solid stone

EARTH'S CORE
liquid iron
solid iron

55

in it, people walk around on it, and moles and worms live there. Subways whoosh around inside it, buildings stand on top of it, and ancient treasures are hidden in it.

The Earth's crust is not one complete piece. It is made up of large and small plates, like shards. These fragments of the Earth's crust are thickest at the Himalayas, about twenty-five miles. That sounds like a lot, but in comparison to the deeper layers of the Earth, it isn't much. If the Earth were as small as an apple, the crust would be thinner than its skin. And under the oceans, the Earth's crust is even thinner: about five miles at most.[3]

The Earth's Mantle

Now it really is getting hot under your feet. In the Earth's mantle, you will probably come across a thick layer of magma first. This is melted stone, just like lava. You know, the stuff that comes out of volcanoes. But as long as it's still in the ground, lava is called magma. It's the same gloopy mass of melted stone, though, with a temperature of 2,400 degrees.[4] As the top layer of the Earth's mantle is so gloopy, the Earth's crust above it is not entirely fixed. It is basically floating on a sea of magma.

Deeper inside the Earth's mantle, the stone is no longer liquid. This is because the layer above it is pressing down so heavily that everything has become harder. Just like the sand on a path where lots of people walk is harder than the surrounding sand.

The Earth's Core

If we keep digging to 1,800 miles under your feet, we'll find ourselves in a deep bath of boiling iron. By that point, we'll have left the Earth's mantle behind and we'll be in the outermost part of the Earth's core.[5] It's hot enough there to melt iron. As the iron is liquid, it slowly flows around. This makes the Earth function like a giant magnet and is the reason why compass needles all over the world point to the North Pole.

The inner core is made of the same material as the outer core. Only it's not liquid, but solid. As with the Earth's mantle, the pressure inside is so high that the iron becomes solid again. So the inner core of the Earth is a big iron marble, with a temperature of more than 9,000 degrees. I think your shovel will probably have melted by now.

But How Do We Know All of This?

Scientists obviously don't simply start digging a hole in the front yard. They have to study the vibrations of earthquakes and explosions. These are known as seismic waves. By measuring the speed and direction of the waves, you can work out what kind of material is deep inside the Earth.

A LIGHT SHOW AT THE POLES

Sometimes charged particles of the sun cause fairy-tale polar lights. Because of the Earth's magnetic field, these particles can only enter the atmosphere above the North Pole and the South Pole. The collision with the atmosphere releases energy in the form of gracefully dancing lights in the colors green, blue, purple, and red.

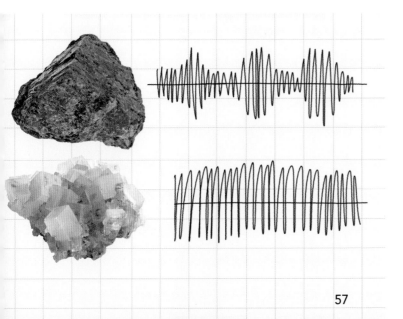

The record for the deepest hole in the world goes to the Russian town of Kola. They started in 1970, aiming to drill to a depth of 49,000 feet. Every time the drill head went a chunk deeper, the Russians attached a new rod of metal. They went on doing this for twenty-two years, and then the ground became too hot for the drill head. They eventually got stuck at 40,230 feet—not even in the Earth's mantle.[6]

SURFING ON MAGMA

How often do you cut your nails? Or are you more of a nail biter? Snipper or biter: if you don't do anything, your nails will grow about one inch a year. As quickly as Europe is drifting away from North America. Because every year the distance between Amsterdam and New York grows by about one inch.[7] At the same time, Africa is moving closer and closer to Europe. In millions of years, the Mediterranean Sea will have sealed up and the distance between Amsterdam and New York will be vast.

BOILING FOUNTAINS

Dozens of tourists stand intently staring at a steaming puddle of water. The local guide watches with confidence. And sure enough, the water comes spurting out of the Earth with a whole lot of force behind it. Geysers like this can be found in only a few places in the world. They happen when magma heats the groundwater until it's so hot that it bursts out through a hole in the ground.

Poor Alfred

If you look closely at the world map, you'll see that some parts of the world fit together very nicely. For example, the coastline of South America fits the coastline of Africa perfectly. The German scientist Alfred Wegener thought that too. He was one of the first to say that the Earth's crust was not fixed and was not a whole unit.[8]

People one hundred years ago found that hard to believe. The continents weren't ships that sailed the oceans, were they? Most people just laughed at poor Wegener, even when he discovered that the same kinds of fossils could be found on both coasts—for example, fossils of the Mesosaurus, a swimming reptile that could not possibly have swum across the ocean. That had to mean that Africa and South America had been stuck together at the time of the dinosaurs. But then how did they drift apart?

Conveyor Belt

Alfred Wegener could not imagine what force could have been behind the movement of the continents: plate tectonics. However, more than thirty years after his death, other scientists managed to solve the puzzle. In the middle of the Atlantic Ocean, they found the longest mountain ridge on Earth. Exactly in the middle between Africa and South America, and between Europe and

MID-ATLANTIC RIDGE

THE PLATES MOVE APART
THE SURFACE TEARS

MAGMA COMES UP

MAGMA SOLIDIFIES,
MAKING NEW ROCK

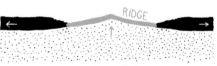

THE SEABED GROWS

North America.[9] Here, deep under the water, the Earth's plates move apart. This allows magma to rise up. As the magma cools, new stone forms and the plates grow larger. So the ocean floor becomes bigger and bigger. And Africa and South America are moving farther and farther apart, as if they're on two conveyor belts, moving in different directions.

250 MILLION YEARS AGO

There are other cracks in the Earth's crust, where the plates are growing. But the Earth is not getting bigger. So there must also be places where the Earth's crust is disappearing. That's right: where two plates meet, the heavier plate slides beneath the lighter one. The deeper the heavy plate goes, the hotter it gets. Eventually the stone melts and merges again with the Earth's mantle. In millions of years' time, it will come back up again and serve as a conveyor belt somewhere else.

NOW

Europe-Africa-Asia

If you rewind the history of the Earth, you will see that continents like Africa, America, Europe, and Asia have already been on quite a journey. Sometimes they were scattered all over the globe and sometimes cozily snuggled together at the South Pole. Around 250 million years ago, they were all

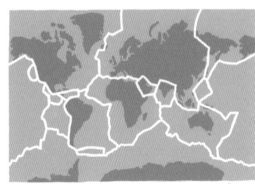

OCEAN AND CONTINENTS ARE ON PLATES.

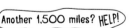

Another 1,500 miles? HELP!

South America ← ATLANTIC OCEAN → Africa

joined together in the supercontinent Pangea. Slowly, the plates, with the continents and the oceans on them, drifted apart. The result is our modern world. Even that is only temporary, though. In millions of years' time, the world will look very different again. Possibly people will be living on a massive continent again, made up of Europe, Africa, Asia, and Australia. You'd be able to walk all the way from China to Australia.

If you quickly speed up the history of the Earth, you'll see that we're all sitting on a few huge rafts and surfing over a hot layer of magma. The world is made up of seven large tectonic plates and around ten smaller ones. They combine to form a jigsaw puzzle in permanent motion. Where plates move apart or come together, mountains and volcanoes are formed. That's where most earthquakes happen too.

ON TOP OF A COLLISION

Okay, so the continents don't stay still. That is, of course, asking for problems. Imagine Africa and Europe are cars heading straight for each other without braking. The drivers of Africa yell: "Watch out for that continent!" But it's too late. The drivers of Europe scream and throw their hands in the air. *Bang!* They crash into each other. The front of Europe is completely crumpled. Today, lots of people hike and ski in those crumples. They're called the Alps.

Pushing and Squeezing

Mountains develop because of motion in the Earth's plates. Plates move toward, away from, and past one another. If two plates are moving toward each other, they have a

problem. Sometimes one plate is much heavier. Then it slides under the other one. But if the plates are around the same weight, they can only go one way: up. Open up this book and push against the sides, and you'll see the same thing happening. That's how the Alps were formed. Or rather: that is how the Alps are still forming, because the collision between the African plate and the European plate is still going on. If you are standing on top of such a mountain, you are standing right on top of a collision. And yet the Alps are hardly growing now, as the little bits that are added every year are worn away by ice, water, and wind.

Shells in the Mountains

You might find it hard to believe that the mountaintops of the Alps are made out of the seabed of days gone by. Then you really should get out there with a good fossil hunter. With a bit of luck, you'll find fossils of fish, shells, and sea urchins high up in the mountains. You can even come across entire coral reefs up there.[10] That's clear evidence that the mountains are pushed-up bits of Earth. Many older civilizations and religions have tried to explain these fossils by connecting them to a major flood, like the one in the story about Noah's ark. According to these stories, the fossils are left over from a time when the water was higher than the mountaintops. But that would take a whole lot of water and a whole lot of time.

India as an Island

You'll also find shells and corals on the highest mountain in the world. That is Mount Everest, at 29,029 feet, about two and a half miles higher than the highest Alpine summit, Mont Blanc. Mount Everest is in the Himalayas, on the border of Pakistan, India, Nepal, and China. In the Himalayas and the Karakorams, also in central Asia, there are thirteen other mountains that are more than 26,247 feet high. They are called the Eight-Thousanders because they are all over 8,000 meters tall.[11] A normal human being is incapable of breathing there. That's why most mountain climbers who go that high have to take oxygen with them. Even so, they don't all survive the climb. But the ones who do reach the top are standing on a former seabed. The tops of the Himalayas are made of limestone, a rock that originates in the sea, made from skeletons, shells, and other remains of sea life.[12] Sixty million years before, that limestone was still lying around on the bottom of the sea. A warm sea, full of fish and other strange creatures that died out long ago. In those days, India was not yet connected to the rest of Asia; it was an enormous island in the ocean. But the plate on which India is situated moved to the north at a

6,000 YEARS

In 1654, Archbishop James Ussher worked out that God had created the Earth on October 23, 4004 BCE.[15] He didn't know exactly when, but it was sometime in the evening. In those days, many more people believed that the world could not be older than around 6,000 years, because that was in line with the Bible. Even today, there are some religious people who think the Earth is that young. They explain the fossils in the ground as remains from the biblical flood.

But, of course, 6,000 years is not long enough to allow mountains to develop, layers of earth to tilt, and species to develop and become extinct. That takes time, lots and lots of time. Modern techniques have been used to calculate that the Earth is around 4.6 billion years old. So Ussher was only 4,599,993,996 years off . . .

speed of about two inches per year—and then sped up to almost six inches per year. Around 50 million years ago, India collided with Asia.[13] And Asia did not get out of the way, so the stone could go in only one direction. That's right—up! That was the start of the Himalayas. The collision slowed India down a bit, but it's still moving north. Because of the way India is pushing, the Himalayas grow just under half an inch every year.[14] So the highest mountaintops in the world get a little higher every year.

The Ring of Fire

So, the Himalayas have the highest mountains. And which range of mountains comes next? The Andes in South America. The record holder is the mountain Aconcagua in Argentina at 22,841 feet. But what about if you empty the Pacific Ocean? Then you would see a much higher mountain range. It is as if the Andes simply continue under the water. Off the west coast of South America, there is an immense depth: a trench. In some places, that trench is more than 26,000 feet deep.[16] So, from the bottom of the trench to the top of the Andes, it is around 49,000 feet.

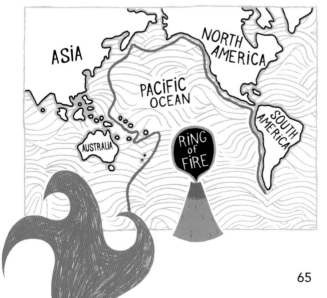

The trench off the coast of South America has the same origins as the mountains of the Andes. Here, too, two sliding plates are involved. But one plate is much heavier than the other. So the plate with the ocean on it is sliding beneath the plate with the land on it. This has formed a deep gorge off the coast. The land rises, and mountains are formed, as in the Alps and the Himalayas. But there is more going on here. In the Andes, many mountains are not just mountains. They are mountains that, all of a sudden, can become a chunk smaller. Mountains that can grow feet in a day. Mountains that terrify people. That's right, we're talking about volcanoes. The whole coast of the Pacific Ocean is full of them. That's why it's sometimes called the Ring of Fire.[17]

1. **Mount Everest**
Nepal and Tibet, 29,029 feet
Highest mountain in Asia—
and the world

2. **Aconcagua**
Argentina, 22,841 feet[18]
Highest mountain in South
America

3. **Denali**[19]
United States, 20,310 feet[20]
Highest mountain in North
America

4. **Kilimanjaro**
Tanzania, 19,341 feet[21]
Highest mountain in Africa

5. **Mount Elbrus**
Russia, 18,510 feet[22]
Highest mountain in Europe

6. **Mount Vinson**
Antarctica, 16,066 feet[23]
Highest mountain in
Antarctica

7. **Puncak Jaya**
Indonesia, 16,024 feet[24]
Highest mountain in Oceania,
the region that includes
Australia and Micronesia

8. **Mont Blanc**
France, 15,771 feet[25]
Highest mountain in the Alps

9. **Matterhorn**
Switzerland, 14,692 feet[26]
Famous mountain in the Alps

10. **Etna**
Italy, 10,900 feet[27]
Highest active volcano in
Europe

11. **Uluru**
Australia, 2,831 feet[28]
Famous rock (Ayers Rock)

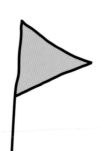

EXPLODING MOUNTAINS

Around sixty miles under your feet, it's hellish![29] A gloopy, glowing mass of stone flows there: magma. And heat always wants to rise. Just take a look at the steam rising from

a boiling kettle. It makes sense, then, that lava comes up out of the ground in some places. It can happen very calmly, like a slow river of bubbling orange syrup, but it can also be a terrible, destructive volcanic eruption.

Saturday, August 11, 1883

Between the Indonesian islands of Sumatra and Java lies the island of Krakatoa. On the island there are three volcanic craters, one of which is half a mile high. Most people call Krakatoa a dormant, or sleeping, volcano. But all that means is that it has not erupted for some time. On Saturday, August 11, 1883, scientists are concerned, as earthquakes have regularly been happening near the volcanoes for a couple months already. And steam is coming from the northern crater. Sometimes there are explosions that you can hear all the way to Jakarta, Indonesia.[30]

On August 11, Captain H. J. G. Ferzenaar is the last human to go to Krakatoa. He sees that lots of new little craters have formed and that the entire island is covered with a thick layer of ash. He advises others not to visit the island for the time being. Sounds like a good recommendation . . . [31]

Sunday, August 26, 1883

A column of black ash, about twenty miles in height, is hanging above the island. There is one eruption after another. Even far out at sea, the ash is raining down on ships.

Monday, August 27, 1883

In the morning, there are four devastating eruptions. The last one can be heard over 3,000 miles away in Africa. It bursts the eardrums of sailors there. Krakatoa is tearing apart. Ash rises 50 miles into the sky. Much of the mountain sinks into the sea, and the hole that remains fills with water. Tidal waves, about 100 feet high, wash villages and cities off the map. Steamships are picked up and smashed down again miles away. Water levels rise all the way to the North Sea. More than 36,000 people die.

Tuesday, August 28, 1883

Krakatoa is still. There are just a few little mud pools still bubbling away. The dust that filled the air darkens the sun. This will disturb the global climate for years. The year after the eruption, the average temperature on Earth is a couple degrees lower than normal.

Monday, August 11, 1930

Forty-seven years later. On the site of Krakatoa, things have been rumbling for a while. But now a new island actually begins to emerge. More lava is spouting than the sea can break up. The island is growing day by day. By now it is over 650 feet high.[32] The Indonesians call the volcanic island Anak Krakatau, the Child of Krakatoa.

Explosive Volcanoes

There are different types of volcanoes. Krakatoa, for example, is an explosive volcano. But you'd probably already realized that. Such volcanoes are usually created when heavy plates move under lighter plates. With Krakatoa, that's the heavy plate that the Indian Ocean lies on. So this ocean floor slides down under the land. There's a lot of seawater within the plate. The plate melts in the hot mantle of the Earth: the stone becomes magma, and the seawater becomes water vapor. Because of the heat, this mixture wants to rise, and it accumulates in the magma chamber. If it can't go anywhere, the pressure rises higher and higher—like in a can of soda that you've just shaken. Suddenly, with a bang, the magma finds a way out. The higher the pressure, the bigger the volcanic explosion.

An explosive volcano like Krakatoa is known as a stratovolcano. You can recognize them by their steep slopes of layers of lava and ash. The lava from a stratovolcano is very tough. That means it doesn't flow as far away and so a steep slope forms. Stratovolcanoes are found mainly along the edges of the Pacific Ocean—the Ring of Fire—as one plate slides under another there. But they can also be found in other places. Mount Vesuvius in Italy is one example. This was created when the African plate slid under the European plate. Stratovolcanoes are more explosive than other volcanoes, and therefore more dangerous. Almost 2,000 years ago, Vesuvius exploded and caused thousands of deaths in and around Pompeii.[33] For centuries, the area was covered in a thick layer of ash. Since then, much of the city

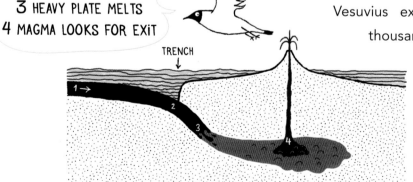

1 PLATES MOVE
2 HEAVY PLATE SLIDES BENEATH LIGHT PLATE
3 HEAVY PLATE MELTS
4 MAGMA LOOKS FOR EXIT

TRENCH

has been dug up, and you can clearly see what it looked like in Roman times.

Slightly Friendlier Volcanoes

Do you remember that longest mountain ridge on Earth, the one in the middle of the Atlantic Ocean? The plates there are not sliding under each other, but apart. There's magma coming up there too. That's how the entire mountain ridge was formed, in fact. There are lots of volcanoes in it, underwater volcanoes. When an underwater volcano rises out of the sea, an island is created. That has happened around Iceland, too, where the mountain ridge rises above water. Iceland is about the size of Kentucky, but it has 130 volcanoes.[34] Many of the volcanoes in Iceland are shield volcanoes. These volcanoes are a little friendlier than stratovolcanoes. Their magma contains fewer gases, can come out more easily, and so does not build up as much pressure. The lava of a shield volcano is also a lot more liquid than in a stratovolcano. It is more like maple syrup as compared to molasses. The lava flows much farther before setting. That is why a shield volcano is a lot less steep, so it resembles a round knight's shield lying there in the landscape.

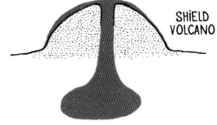

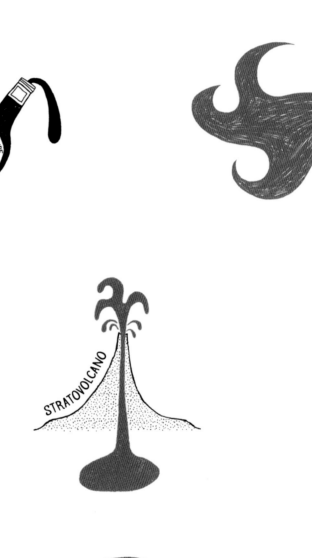

STRATOVOLCANO

SHIELD VOLCANO

While the stratovolcano likes to keep everything bottled up, the shield volcano is a real chatterbox. Its mouth is always open, with the lava running out like a stream of words. Meanwhile, the stratovolcano has it all corked up until the next eruption.

Living Near a Volcano

Volcanoes are dangerous, as we saw in the case of Krakatoa. So why do people live there? That's because the soil around a volcano is very fertile, thanks to the substances in the volcanic ash. So the fields around a volcano often produce good crops. For many farmers, this is more important than the risk they are running, particularly if they're poor, as in Central America and Indonesia.

The Three Biggest Dangers

Scientists kind of saw the eruption of Krakatoa coming, but a volcanic explosion is usually hard to predict. Even a volcano that's been sleeping for thousands of years can suddenly wake up. And you'd better make sure you get out of its way.

There are three major dangers.

Volcanoes in Everyone's Backyards

ZZZ
JUST RECOVERING

DORMANT VOLCANO

You may think volcanoes are only in certain parts of the world, but they are everywhere. They might not be too active, but that doesn't mean they're dead. The Puy-de-Dôme (pronounced: pwee duh dom) is in the Auvergne in France. This volcano last erupted around 7,600 years ago. But before that, this area was active for 20 million years. So why shouldn't it erupt again?[39]

The Eifel in Germany is another surprising site. There are even bubbles of gas rising in the nearby Laacher See, where tourists swim; they're evidence of the volcanic activity in this old volcanic crater. The Eifel's last volcanic eruption, about 10,000 years ago, spewed rocks that still litter the ground.[40] And it's quite common for a volcano to be quiet for 10,000 years between two eruptions. So it's possible that you'll live to experience another eruption of this volcano.

The Netherlands also has a volcano. It's called Zuidwal and is deep in the ground underneath the Wadden Sea. People who take a boat from the town of Harlingen to the island of Vlieland sail over it.

1. Lava is very hot—at least 1,400 degrees, but it can be as much as 2,200 degrees.[35] That's about five times hotter than the oven you put your pizza in. The good thing about lava is that it doesn't flow too quickly. Your grandma could probably run faster. But the bad thing is that it's almost impossible to stop. Lava from shield volcanoes just keeps on flowing, and it sets fire to everything in its path. For days, weeks, sometimes months, destroying everything it comes into contact with. Once lava has cooled, it leaves behind a thick layer of rock.

2. Volcanoes blow enormous clouds of ash miles into the sky. These glowing hot clouds contain lumps of stone but also really fine, sharp particles of dust. In 2010, Eyjafjallajökull erupted on Iceland. A small part of the island was covered in ash. But most of the ash blew toward Europe where hardly any planes could fly for days, since the ash might get into the engines.[36] The ash clouds get really nasty, though, when they collapse under their own weight. This causes a deadly avalanche of ash, lava, and rocks, which carries away everything in its path and cooks people and animals alive. The temperature in such an avalanche can get up to 1,400 degrees, and its speed can be well over one hundred miles an hour.[37]

3. Volcanoes that are covered with a thick layer of ice and snow form an extra danger. If that ice melts all at once, a terrible river of mud runs down the mountain. On the way, it carries along all of the debris from the volcanic explosion. In 1985, a river like that covered the Colombian city of Armero in a layer of mud that was 165 feet thick. At least 20,000 people did not survive.[38]

The volcano is over 3,000 feet high, and it was discovered in 1970 when people started drilling there for gas and noticed a slightly higher temperature. Around 150 million years ago, during the late Jurassic, the volcano was still active. After that, it was covered in a few miles of limestone, sand, and a thin layer of sea. That's why we never hear anything from it these days.[41]

SHAKING EARTH

On March 11, 2011, Japan moved a few feet. This happened during the most severe earthquake ever measured in the country. The earthquake took place at sea and caused a tidal wave sixty-five feet high: a tsunami. In total, there were more than 20,000 deaths, and thousands of people were never found. Entire villages and cities were destroyed, and there was a terrible accident with a nuclear reactor.[42]

With a Jolt

The Earth's crust is made up of different plates, and they are moving in different directions. That causes a whole lot of pushing and shoving. It's a bit like when

$$n = \frac{2}{3} \log \left(\frac{E}{2} \right) - 3$$

CHARLES RICHTER

1935

one class is trying to get in through a door at the same time as another class is trying to get out. Sometimes you can't budge, but then you push a little harder, and you suddenly shoot through the doorway. What a relief!

That's what happens with the Earth's crust too. The plates push into, and against one another, and get stuck behind each other. And they keep on pushing until they can move. So sometimes a plate shoots forward with a big jolt: an earthquake.

What It Feels Like

Imagine you're at school. The ground starts vibrating. There's a huge noise like a massive truck driving by. Really, really close. And faster and faster. Your stomach feels weird. Everyone dives under their desks. The walls shake. Glasses clink. Your teacher pushes with all her weight against a cupboard so that it won't fall over. Lights rattle. Windows break. Computers fall off the desks. Books tumble from the shelves. Suddenly, you can hear your classmates screaming. The rumbling of the ground gradually dies away. Cautiously, you come out from under your desk and look around. What a mess!

Once you're outside, the chaos is even worse. There's glass all over the streets. There's a worrying smell of gas in the air. Trees have snapped in two. Telephone poles have collapsed like houses of cards. An apartment building has fallen over. Rusty bars are sticking out of concrete like bones. Water spurts from broken water pipes. Cars have come to a stop in the strangest places. Bridges have fallen apart. The asphalt is full of cracks, some of them big enough to swallow a car.

It Could Be Worse

Every year millions of earthquakes happen in the world. Most of those quakes are very small, so small that hardly anyone even notices. But about 500,000 each year can be detected by machines, 100,000 felt by humans, and 100 cause damage.[43] A few times a year there's a quake that makes the news. That means it's quite a bit more serious.

The RICHTER SCALE

1 YOU WON'T FEEL THIS VIBRATION.

2 DO YOU SEE THE LIGHT GENTLY SWAYING?

3 LIKE A TRUCK GOING BY.

4 WINDOWS CRACK, AND SMALL OBJECTS MOVE.

5 FURNITURE MOVES.

6 CRACKS APPEAR IN WALLS.

7 THE EARTH OPENS UP.

8 DAMAGE TO BRIDGES AND BUILDINGS.

9 EVERYTHING SHAKES AND TREMBLES. NOTHING REMAINS STANDING.

We use the Richter scale to indicate just how serious. For example, the news about the earthquake on March 11, 2011, sounded something like this:

> Japan has been hit by a very severe earthquake, with a force of nine on the Richter scale.
>
> The epicenter of the quake was about seventy-five miles to the east of Sendai, in the Pacific Ocean.

By the *epicenter*, they meant the spot directly above the place in the Earth's crust where the quake occurred. From there, the shock waves spread out all around. A force of nine on the Richter scale is pretty powerful. On average that kind of earthquake happens only a few times each century.[44]

The Richter scale is a bit of a weird scale. You might think that a force nine earthquake is just a bit more powerful than an earthquake of force eight. But that's not the case. One extra point means ten times more powerful, while two extra points means a hundred times more powerful.

About five years after the earthquake in Japan, on February 25, 2016, there was a small earthquake in Oklahoma. It had a force of four on the Richter scale before the US Geological Survey downgraded it to a 3.6. So, the earthquake in Japan was 100,000 times more powerful than the one there. Recently, Oklahoma has been experiencing thousands of earthquakes like that or smaller because, many experts think, of the injection of wastewater from oil and natural gas production into the ground.[45] Even so, people report feeling some of those quakes. You can only imagine the consequences of the earthquake in Japan, which was so much more powerful.

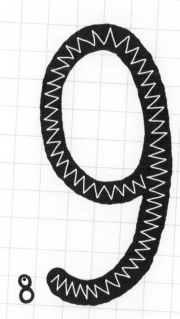

Used to Earthquakes

In places such as the Netherlands and Spain, there are no big earthquakes. This is because those countries are far away from the edges of the plates. Along those edges is where the most serious earthquakes happen, as that's where the pieces of the Earth's crust are pushing and shoving. So Japan is quite used to earthquakes. That country is directly on the Ring of Fire, the edge of the Pacific Ocean, where there are so many volcanoes, and so many earthquakes happen. As with the Andes, the Pacific plate slides under the plates that the land lies on. With the usual consequences: off the coast of Japan, there is a trench over six miles in depth, Japan is teeming with volcanoes, and every year people can feel up to 2,000 earthquakes, many being earthquakes magnitude six or above.[46]

So, most serious quakes occur in the Ring of Fire. But they also happen in other places: wherever two or more plates come together. So, for example, in Italy, Turkey, Pakistan, Indonesia, and the Caribbean.

Disastrous Consequences

The number of victims in an earthquake largely depends on two factors: how many people live in the affected area and how well their houses are built. In wealthy countries such as the United States, Italy, and Japan, buildings are constructed to be extra sturdy in areas where earthquakes are common. Countries like Haiti, however, do not have enough money to do that. In an earthquake in 2010, more than 300,000 people lost their lives; that is almost as many as the number of inhabitants of the city of Cincinnati. And 1.5 million people—more than all the residents of San Diego—lost their homes.[47]

In a serious earthquake underwater, the greatest danger is often the tsunami, as happened with the quake in Japan. A tsunami is a tidal wave that originates in the place where the Earth's crust sinks or rises. It's easy enough to imitate what happens then. Fill your bathtub, put a few dolls on the edge, and climb

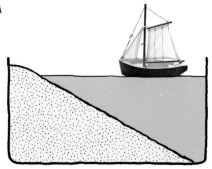

into the bath with force nine on the Richter scale. Suddenly standing up in the bath will do the trick too. From the epicenter, a wave of water will spread in every direction. Close to the coast, the water becomes more shallow, so the wave has to rise up. In Japan, it grew to a height of more than sixty-five feet in some places, and the water came about six miles inland.[48] Residents of the affected area had half an hour to escape. Then a gigantic amount of water washed away boats, cars, and houses. If you type *Sendai tsunami* into YouTube, you'll see how just devastating the tidal wave was. Debris from Japan is still washing up on US shores— along with hitchhiking Japanese animals. For example, five striped beakfish were born and raised on a boat that got ripped away from its dock and drifted for two years and four thousand miles till it bumped against Washington State.[49]

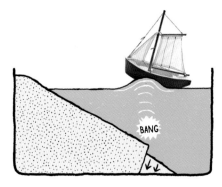

An earthquake itself is actually not that dangerous. If you're standing in the middle of a field somewhere when an earthquake hits, then you should survive. Most of the dangers are because of the consequences: collapsing buildings, leaking gas pipes, tsunamis, diseases that break out because of a lack of clean water. And in Japan, there was an extra danger: a nuclear power station was damaged by the tsunami. People were no longer in control of what happened inside the power station. Substances were released that can cause cancer. So for the next few decades, no one will be able to live anywhere near the power station.

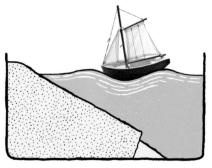

A TIDAL WAVE IS BORN

WATER, WATER EVERYWHERE

4

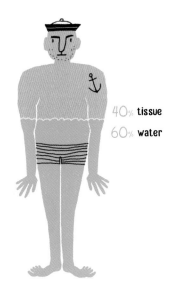

40% tissue
60% water

A WATERY PLANET

Waterslides, watersports, water paint, watermelon, waterworks, water pipes, water pistols, waterpower, water birds . . . our lives are drenched with water. That's no surprise, really, because you may know the facts already: your body is at least 60 percent water, and the Earth's surface is over 70 percent water.

It's Hailing; It's Hailing

Scientists can't be absolutely certain, but they think that most of our water ended up on Earth as the result of a bombardment of ice meteorites.[1] It must have been a whole load of meteorites. We're talking about millions of chunks of ice over millions of years. And they must have been very big meteorites. Some of them would have been as big as Australia. Well, that's what the scientists think. As soon as the lumps of ice hit the Earth, the heat of the Earth's young surface melted them.

All that water has combined to cover most of our planet. It is in the oceans, lakes, rivers, icebergs, raindrops, garden hoses, swimming pools, and cans of soda. We won't be getting any more water. So we have to be careful with it, because life is impossible without water. Now I can hear you thinking: Hey, but the whole planet's full of water, isn't it? That's right. And: Hey, then that must be more than enough? Well, no, it isn't. Because more and more people are coming along every day, and they need more and more water. And most water isn't suitable for use as drinking water. The vast majority of it is salt water, and nearly all of the rest is frozen.

The Earth as a Bathtub

Imagine if all the water on Earth could fit into a bathtub. Fill it up, nice and full. Then take out four liter-sized bottles of water. The rest of the bath is salt water, and so it is undrinkable. We have to make do with just those four bottles. Oh, and the water in three of those bottles is frozen. It is frozen solid in ice caps in Greenland, Antarctica, and elsewhere. On the top of one of the frozen bottles, there is a little splash of meltwater. That is all the water in rivers, lakes, and clouds. Luckily we have a fourth bottle of fresh water. That is the water that is in the

FRESH CLOUDS

We call it fresh water to distinguish it from salt water. You can't drink salt water, and it's not good for most plants either. The seas are salty because they contain salts from the seabed and from underwater volcanoes. When seawater evaporates, it leaves those salts behind. So, the clouds are made of fresh water, just like rain, snow, and the rivers that take this water back to the sea.

3% fresh
97% salt

PURE WATER

82

ground, which is where we get most of our drinking water from. However, we can't just pump up all of that groundwater. Partly because it's difficult to reach, but also because the soil can't be allowed to dry out.

ENDLESS WATER

Are you enjoying a nice cup of tea or a glass of lemonade? There's a good chance that it contains particles that were once peed out by a stegosaurus, and also bits of Michael Jackson's drops of sweat. Some of the particles might even have been in the iceberg that made the *Titanic* sink. Water molecules go through all kinds of things. They freeze, melt, go up into the air, and fall to Earth again. That is the cycle of water.

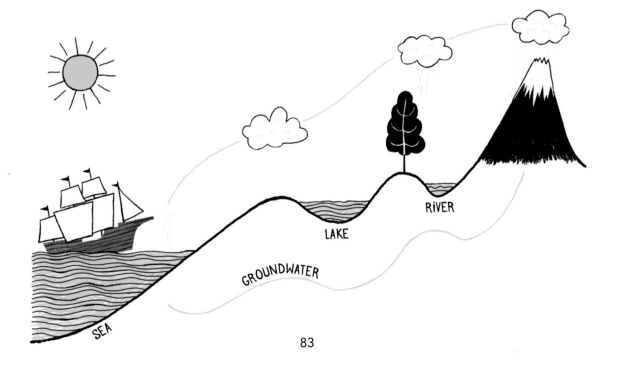

83

From Ice to Cloud

Put a container of water into the freezer, and it'll turn into ice. If you let the ice melt, it'll turn back into liquid water. Heat the water in the kettle, and it'll evaporate. A little cloud will appear above the kettle. You might think that the cloud is water vapor, but you can't actually see water vapor. The water vapor floats in the air between the kettle and the cloud, invisibly. The cloud contains tiny little droplets of water: the water vapor that has already cooled down. Clouds in the sky are also made up of water droplets and of ice. The water vapor floats in the air between the ground and the clouds.

The Journey of Water

The Earth does not have a kettle or a freezer. And yet the cycle of water works at its best here. The sun warms the water of oceans, rivers, lakes, and other wet places. This makes the water rise in the form of vapor. You can't see it, but the air around you is full of it. Higher in the air, it gets cooler, and the water vapor becomes liquid again; the droplets float through the sky as clouds. They collide with one another, become heavier, and fall to the ground. The rain or snow falls into the water and onto the land. In places where it is cold, the snow stays lying on the ground. For days, years, centuries, or even longer. In other places, the water sinks into the ground. Some of it goes to the plants, some of it seeps through to the groundwater, and some of it flows into streams and rivers. The rivers take the water back to the sea. However, it isn't always that simple.

Water and Its Roundabout Routes

There is also water that ends up at the bottom of the ocean and does not evaporate for thousands of years. There is water that is used to make popsicles that stay in the freezer for years. There is water that is sucked up by a cucumber plant. There is water in your stomach, which your body uses to make blood. There is water that falls in a tropical rainforest and goes straight back into the air because of the heat. There is water that ends up in a waterbed and spends years splashing about under your snoring parents. There is water in the storm that goes right through your summer coat. There is water that has been stuck in the ice of Antarctica for years. There is water vapor that you breathe out onto a window

SPOT THE SiMiLARiTY

(WATER)

and write your name in. There is water in fluffy clouds; squirting, soaking water toys; ice cubes . . . Water is all around you, and all of it is part of this endless cycle of water.

WATERY WORDS

An **ocean** is big and deep and lies between different continents. There are five of them on Earth.

A **sea** is much smaller and shallower and lies on the edge of an ocean or is surrounded by land.

So a sea can also be the shallow edge of an ocean.

A **lake** is a small or large area of fresh water, surrounded by land.

A **river** is a length of fresh water going from high to low.

A **stream** is like a river but much smaller and shallower.

A **canal** is dug by humans. As a result, it is much straighter than a river.

85

THE ETERNAL LiFE OF STONE

Hey, if those mountains just keep on growing, why isn't the world full of incredibly high mountains? Then Mount Everest and Denali will be twice as high at some point in the future, won't they? And won't the Tour de France cyclists in the year 2000015 have a climb of over fifty miles?

Rubble

Mountains don't just grow. They also wear down. Soil people walk on today may consist of material that wore away from mountains. Ex-mountains, in other words. For example, those in North and Central Europe live on the rubble of mountains, even when they live in the valleys. Those mighty Alps are broken down just as quickly as they rise up.

That little grain of sand that you have somewhere in the seam of your pants pocket (go on, feel it—it's really there) was once part of a giant rock that only mountain goats, eagles, and superconfident climbers could reach. How did that little grain of sand make it so far? Hey, why don't we ask it?

MY LIFE AS A GRAIN OF SAND

I can still remember it so clearly. It all began deep in the Earth. Man, it was hot there. So hot that I couldn't tell what was me and what was my neighbor. We were all one big, flowing mass of stone. Sure, it was nice and cozy. But at a certain point, it all got way too busy in there. It felt like everyone was pushing and shoving. Harder and harder. There was nowhere to go. Then, suddenly, we all flew up into the sky. The view was amazing! I could

see where all of my family had ended up over the past centuries. They weren't liquid anymore, but solid. They weren't orange now, but black. Together, they formed a pretty impressive volcano, the one that I'd just been hurled out of. I waved at my grandma, at my second cousin, but they ignored me. Or maybe they just couldn't move.

We all landed on a slope of the volcano. Suddenly everyone started calling me lava.

"Excuse me?" I said. "I'm magma!" But they all just laughed at me.

"Out here, we're all lava. Welcome!"

Very slowly, we flowed on a bit. I became colder and colder. We flowed more and more slowly, until we were stone-cold. Everyone turned black. And finally, I was stuck there.

I have no idea how long I lay there like that, but it must have been a good few million years. At first, another layer of hot lava came flowing over me every now and then, but in the end, the volcano stopped doing very much. And the layer of lava rock started to wear down as well, probably because of that awful wind blasting all those rough grains of sand over the mountain. One day, I thought, one day I'll have my revenge.

I have to say that the view got better and better. It seemed like I was getting higher and higher. And it kept getting colder too. That made me shrink. In the daytime, it was warmer, and I expanded. All that shrinking and expanding made little cracks appear in me and around me. Here and there, succulent plants began to grow, their ability to retain water in their leaves helping them survive in the rocky ground. *Oh, that's nice*, I thought. But their tough roots made cracks in the stone. When it rained, water got into the cracks. When it froze, the water became ice. One day I heard a *crack*, and I suddenly found myself rolling down the slope in a lump of stone. Until I splashed into the water. Don't forget: I was much bigger back then than I am now. A rough stone full of holes and corners and edges. I don't know how many grains of sand we eventually turned into, but I haven't seen most of them since.

The water we fell into was a wild mountain river. We bounced from rock to rock, becoming smaller and smaller. The sharpest edges went first. After we'd traveled for a while, the water started moving a lot more slowly. We sank to the bottom and slowly bounced along. When we reached the sea, I was still a pretty rough grain. Then the waves caught hold of me. Just the thought of it makes me feel seasick. They dragged me onto the beach and back again. Onto the beach and back again. Onto the beach and back again. Over and over. But that's what gave me this nice smooth look.

I have to say that I'm happy I ended up in a pocket, because I heard stories in those waves that would make you shudder. Grains falling to the seabed and being crushed flat by other layers. Grains disappearing into a layer with limestone with bits of shell and skeleton. And I even heard of some that went deeper, disappearing under the ground and becoming lava again. The whole cycle beginning all over again. Ugh, what a thought!

A Cycle of Stone

Every stone on Earth, from the tiniest grain of sand to the biggest boulder, is part of an endless cycle. Just like the bottles that you take to be recycled: the glass is broken, the shards are melted, and mixed with other molten glass, and then it's used to make more bottles, which you take to be recycled again. And so it continues.

This cycle of stone is a bit more complicated than glass. And it also takes a lot longer, at least a few million years. Stones also break and disappear beneath other

layers. The pressure causes new stones to form. Layers of stone end up deeper in the Earth. The heat and the pressure make them mix with other stones. Stones that sink deeper eventually melt and become magma. When that magma cools down, it solidifies into stone again.

Cracked!

So, a young stone or rock can just be a piece of cooled-down magma or compressed sand. Changes in temperature make cracks appear in the stone. The roots of plants sometimes get into those cracks and make them bigger. Water can also get into them. When that water freezes, it expands, and the stone can fall apart into pieces. They might call this weathering at school. And if they do, you're lucky, because some teachers call it erosion. But it's only really erosion when those pieces of stone are transported somewhere. Wind, water, and ice take the bits of stone on a long journey.

Howling Wind

The wind takes only the smallest of pieces, of course. But make no mistake: the wind can move entire hills of sand. For example, now and then, desert sand from the Sahara blows high up into the air and travels north. When it rains in Northern Europe, the sand comes down onto the people who live there. The car wash does good business on days like that, because lots of people want to wash the thin red layer of sand off their cars as quickly as possible.

Wind and sand combine to form the perfect sanding machine. Year after year, the wind chases the grains of sand across the landscape. This creates the strangest shapes, particularly with soft stones. Check out pages 92–93 for pictures of the White Desert, Antelope Canyon, or Cappadocia. You really will see the most peculiar landscapes.

Swirling Water

Water is the most important means of transportation for stones. Streams and rivers have broken up entire mountain ranges and carried them to the sea. High in the mountains, the stones are still angular and pretty large, but the water flows quickly there and so is able to carry them. Later on, the mountains become less steep and the water is calmer. The heaviest stones sink to the bottom, while the rest are carried farther on. On the way, they bump and bang into one another, becoming increasingly smaller and smoother. The closer the river gets to the sea, the more slowly the river flows. The more slowly the river flows, the smaller the stones are that sink to the bottom. Only the lightest and hardest bits of stone make it as far as the sea. You'll find mainly clay and sand there, which you can use to make the most beautiful sand sculptures.

LIFE LEAVES ITS MARKS

You can read some of a stone's history in its appearance. A smooth stone was brought here by water and made nice and smooth and round on the way. A rough stone was carried by ice, so it hardly wore out on its travels.

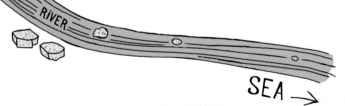

Flowing Ice

In some places around the world, including in the least mountainous places of the United States, you will come across really heavy stones. But wait a second—blocks of stone like that can only come from mountains, can't they? How did they end up in the fields of, say, Yellowstone National Park, which is mostly in Wyoming? That's right—those boulders come from over Tioga Pass in the Sierra Nevada mountains of California. Yellowstone and much of the United States has been covered and uncovered and recovered by glaciers over the millions of years. During the ice age about 20,000 years ago, the glaciers carried along big pieces of rock, known as glacial erratics, which were left behind when the ice melted. Throughout the European continent, the ice of the North Pole expanded south, stopping about halfway across the Netherlands. These glaciers created the signature gentle hills of the Netherlands. Like a bulldozer, they pushed the slabs of frozen ground in front of them.[2]

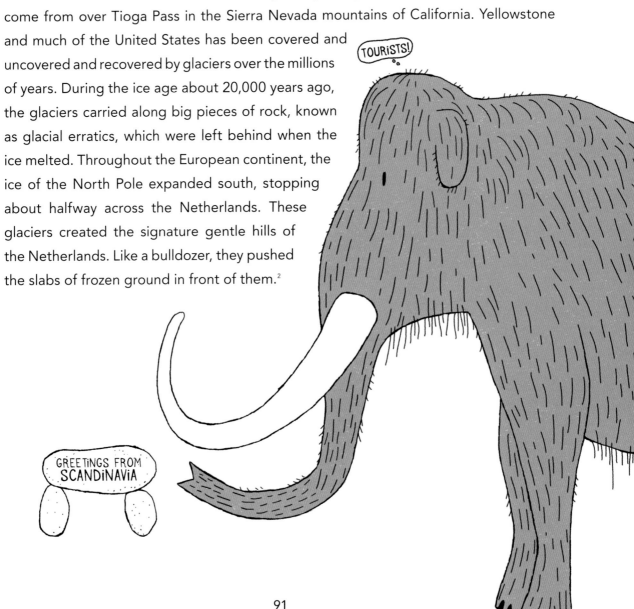

Seven Sisters Cliffs, *England*

Patagonia glacier, *Argentina*

Zanskar and Indus rivers, *Himalayas, India*

EAST
WEST
HOME'S
BEST

Antelope Canyon, *Arizona*

Cappadocia, *Turkey*

Moriane Lake, *Alberta, Canada*

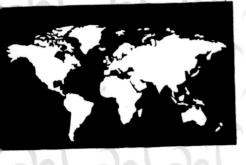

Victoria Falls,
Zambia and Zimbabwe

White Desert, *Egypt*

Torres del Paine, *Chile*

Namibia Desert, *Africa*

Angel Falls, *Venezuela*

Trolltunga, *Norway*

Halong Bay, *Vietnam*

Volcanic mountains, *Iceland*

Uluru, *Australia*

Lena Pillars, *Russia*

TRACES IN THE LANDSCAPE

On the moon, the life of a grain of sand is a lot duller. The footsteps of the first man on the moon are still there in the sand, just as they were on the day they were made, July 21, 1969. This is because there is no wind on the moon to move the grains of sand. There are also no plants to crack the rocks. And most important of all: there is no liquid water, which can wear down entire valleys. Luckily, things are different on our planet. That means we can go skiing, climbing, and rafting.

Visit Amazing Waterfalls

So, there you are, with your knees up against the fence. Tiny droplets blow against your skin and clothes. You're looking down two hundred feet to where the water is hitting the white foaming surface of the river with a deafening noise. Once upon a time, you could just keep on walking where the fence is now. Back then the ground was as high there as it is where you're standing. However, it was made of a different, softer kind of stone.

Waterfalls usually occur at the point where hard stone meets soft stone. Under the force of the river water, the soft variety of stone wears down more quickly. The waterfall slowly moves back, eating away at the rocks it is falling from.

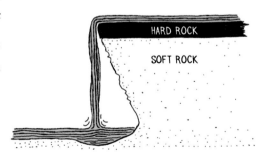
HARD ROCK

SOFT ROCK

Relax on the Most Beautiful Beaches

You gaze idly at the waves. Your hair is dripping onto your towel. Your hand digs a little hollow in the loose sand. The grains keep trickling back into the hole. But then your fingertips touch the firm, wet sand. A grain sticks beneath your nail. If that grain of sand could talk! Marco Polo's and Harry Potter's adventures are boring in comparison. It came here with billions of others, all the way from the mountains. Only the hardest and finest grains of sand made it to the sea, where they dance along with every wave. Some grains of sand stay on the beach, while the sea picks up others and carries them away. But over the course of time, the sea has deposited enough sand for stacks of people to sunbathe, fly kites, and dig little holes in. There was even enough sand left to make dunes—but it was the wind that did that.

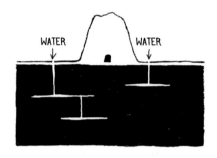

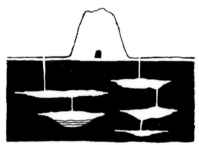

WATER SINKS AND LEAVES CAVITIES BEHIND

Wander Through Mysterious Caves

The rocky path is wet, smooth, and bumpy. The lighting isn't that great. You'd like to take some photographs, but you're afraid of losing sight of the group. And then you'll be wandering around all alone in these dark corridors, deep inside the Earth, surrounded by bats. It's strange to think that there's such a high mountain above your head. A massive lump of limestone. That means that, long ago, this rock was on the bottom of the sea. It is made up of billions of shells and the skeletons of dead sea creatures.

LIMESTONE

Plate tectonics brought this layer of limestone here. In some places, water is coming through the cracks. That makes the limestone dissolve. This can happen up on the surface but also deep in the ground. That's how underground caves and tunnels are made. They're stunningly beautiful to walk through but a terrifying place to get lost.

Descend Fiendish Slopes

Can you feel the tears in your eyes? And the wind in your hair? You're heading down the slope at breakneck speed. On your snowboard, on your racing bike—the choice is yours. Keep your eyes on the way ahead, your mom would say. Otherwise, you'll fly straight into the ravine. If you're really unlucky, you'll roll all the way to the wild river that wore out this valley. Once upon a time, the land here was almost as high as the summits. There wasn't much here for skiers or cyclists back then. It was all just one big plateau.

The melted snow found its way down in winding streams. Those streams carried stones with them, carving the valley out more deeply and joining to form a river that grew larger and larger. Millions of years of flowing water have made the valley as deep as it is now.

YOUNG AND OLD

If you return to the Alps in a few million years' time, you'll see that the peaks are lot blunter. Erosion and weathering break down the mountains that are built up by plate tectonics. This means that old mountain ranges are lower and less jagged than young mountains. Just compare the Ardennes of Belgium to the Alps: The highest Alp is well over 15,700 feet, and most of the Alps have sharp peaks. The highest point of the Ardennes is less than 2,300 feet,[3] and the summits are pretty blunt. But the Ardennes were once about as high and pointy as the Alps. Millions of years in weather and wind have made them shorter and blunter. If Africa had not collided with Europe, they would have disappeared completely.

Climb Steep Walls

So, you know that wall in the climbing gym pretty well, huh? Well, now it's time for the real thing: a steep wall of rock that goes up almost vertically. You're best off with the wall of a glacial valley. A river valley is usually shaped like a V when you look at it straight on. This is because the water always chooses the deepest point. The rocks on the banks crumble from below and fall into the river, creating the steep slopes of the V.

If a thick layer of ice (a glacier) later finds its way into the valley, the V can change into a U, with steep walls and a flat bottom. This is because the ice is not just in the deepest part but across the entire width of the valley. Very slowly, the river of ice flows down the mountain, so slowly that you can barely see the movement. Along the bottom and the sides, the ice drags along lumps of stone, which scour out the valley on all sides. Glaciers can become millions of years old, and so they have plenty of time to carve out the most beautiful walls of rock. Often you can still see the scratches from the ice on them.

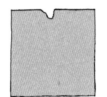

Go White Water Rafting in a Canyon

You can have fun on the river itself too, of course. Go rafting in the Grand Canyon. Let the white water carry you along. Take a look at those steep rock faces and all the colored layers of stone. Over the course of two billion years, they were laid on top of one another, layer by layer. Twenty million years ago, a nice little river babbled its way through here. Plate tectonics lifted the Earth's crust, and gradually the river carved its way deeper into the stone. Eventually it became the vast and wild Colorado River, which cut out a huge gorge, where in some places you can recognize as many as forty layers of rock. And brace yourself, because we're speeding up now.

THE DEEPER, THE OLDER

Let's make a mega club sandwich. Start with a slice of bread. Then a layer of butter. Put a thick slice of cheese on it. Top it with another piece of bread. A bit of mustard, some ham, mayo. More bread, turkey, more cheese, pickles, and another slice of bread. That makes twelve layers, if I counted right. Cut the sandwich in half, like a river cutting through the mountains. Which layer is the oldest one? It's the layer you put down first, of course: the first slice of bread. Followed by the butter and the cheese.

That's what happens with layers of rock in the Earth too. The deeper the layer, the older the rock. That's a good thing to know if you're studying the history of the Earth. A fossil at a depth of sixty feet is usually older than one at a depth of thirty feet. However, that isn't always the case. Tectonic forces sometimes tilt the Earth's crust, or fold it in two, or squeeze it together. Just like the sandwich when you sink your teeth into it.

FRESH MEGA-
MULTI-PROTO-
SANDWICH

1. **Lake Superior**
Borders with the countries of the United States and Canada
31,700 square miles[5]
Largest freshwater lake in surface area

2. **Lake Victoria**
Borders with the countries of Tanzania, Uganda, and Kenya
26,828 square miles[7]
Largest lake in Africa

3. **Lake Baikal**
Borders with the country of Russia
12,200 square miles[6]
Deepest freshwater lake, with largest amount of water

4. **Lake Titicaca**
Borders with the countries of Peru and Bolivia
3,200 square miles
Largest lake in South America and highest lake in the world, at 12,500 feet[8]

5. **Dead Sea**
Borders with Israel, Jordan, and the Palestinian West Bank
394 square miles and dropping
Lowest lake in the world at 1,410 feet below sea level and dropping three feet annually. Also, no fish can live in this body of water due to the high salt content.[9]

6. **Caspian Sea**
Borders with the countries of Russia, Kazakhstan, Turkmenistan, Iran, and Azerbaijan
149,200 square miles[4]
Largest saltwater lake

7. **Loch Ness**
Borders with the country of Scotland
22 square miles[10]
According to some people, the home of the Loch Ness Monster

GOT ONE!

98

Caves

Sometimes a deep hole suddenly appears in the Earth, a sinkhole. This generally happens in limestone areas, where caves also form. Rainwater dissolves the stone and suddenly the ground collapses.

Thousands of years ago, early humans used to sleep in caves. In some places, beautiful wall paintings have been found, usually featuring the animals they hunted.

The water that dissolves limestone can make magnificent caverns with what look like icicles made of rock hanging from the ceiling: stalactites. Where the drops land, pillars form: stalagmites.

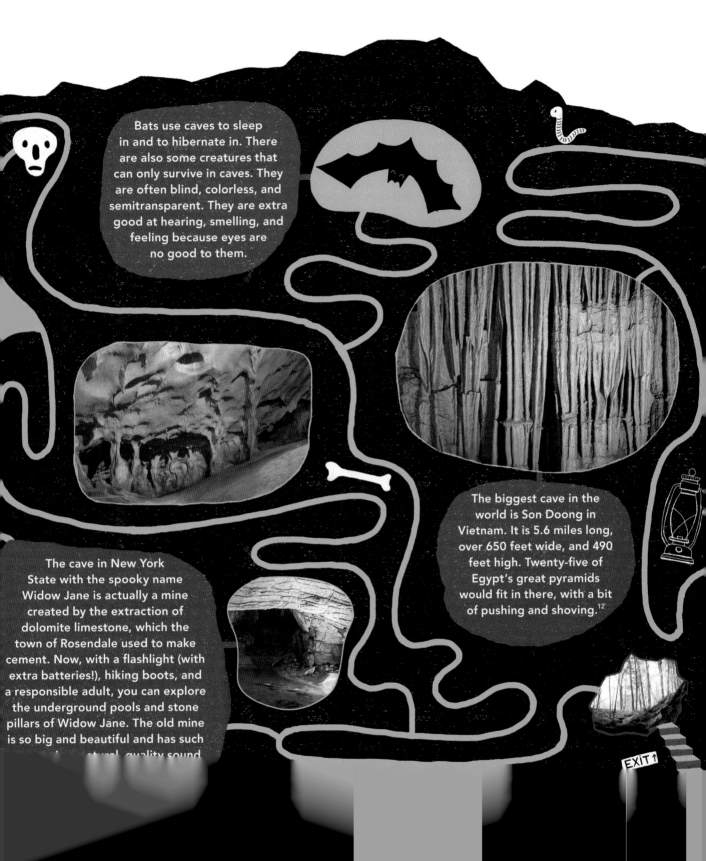

Bats use caves to sleep in and to hibernate in. There are also some creatures that can only survive in caves. They are often blind, colorless, and semitransparent. They are extra good at hearing, smelling, and feeling because eyes are no good to them.

The biggest cave in the world is Son Doong in Vietnam. It is 5.6 miles long, over 650 feet wide, and 490 feet high. Twenty-five of Egypt's great pyramids would fit in there, with a bit of pushing and shoving.[12]

The cave in New York State with the spooky name Widow Jane is actually a mine created by the extraction of dolomite limestone, which the town of Rosendale used to make cement. Now, with a flashlight (with extra batteries!), hiking boots, and a responsible adult, you can explore the underground pools and stone pillars of Widow Jane. The old mine is so big and beautiful and has such

EXIT ↑

TREASURE HUNTERS

Many rocks in the Earth contain incredibly valuable substances with strange names, like bauxite, silicon, strontium . . . Without bauxite, there would be no aluminum to make fast bikes. Thanks to silicon, we have glass, which allows us to look outside, and nice fast computers and cell phones. And strontium creates the greenish glow of those glow-in-the-dark stickers above your bed. How about that?

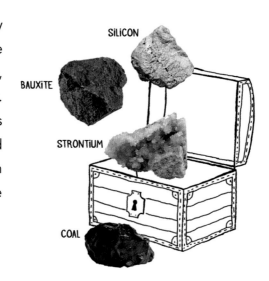

Thanks to Raw Materials

Bauxite, silicon, and strontium are examples of minerals. Every mineral has its own special characteristics. For example, they can be very hard or very magnetic. Most minerals originate in the cycle of stone. Some minerals occur independently—for example, the salt you sprinkle on your egg. Other minerals run all the way through the rock and are difficult to extract. Rocks containing minerals that we can use, we call ores. Together with other useful substances, such as water, wood, and fuels, these minerals are raw natural materials. They're all pieces of the Earth that we have used to build our world. From the very first hut to the skyscrapers of today. Without these resources, we wouldn't have gotten much further than the average baboon.

What Good Is That?

People sift sand and stones for years in the hope of one day finding a lump of gold. You can make pretty jewelry from gold, of course, but it's also practically essential in the latest smartphones.

GOLD

Copper has become so expensive that thieves go out in the middle of the night to steal pipes and statues made of copper. Copper is so valuable because it conducts electricity very well. In the average car in the United States, there are fifty-five pounds of copper wiring; there is three times that much in an electric car.[13]

COPPER

But don't go thinking that minerals are only useful for luxury goods like cars, bicycles, or smartphones. There are also mines where phosphates are extracted, an important ingredient in fertilizer. Fertilizer ensures better harvests and therefore helps to feed an ever-growing population around the world.

Crushed Animals and Plants

There are many other raw materials that people are happy to dig up half a mountain to get at. Using drills, bulldozers, and dynamite, they attack the Earth's crust in thousands of places all over the world. Some of these substances have taken millions of years to develop, but we use them up in a couple centuries. This is certainly true of oil, gas, and coal—also known as fossil fuels. But maybe a better name would be: crushed ancient animals and plants. Because that's actually what they are.

It began even before the dinosaurs roamed the Earth, more than 300 million years ago.[14] The

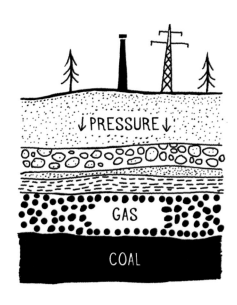

equator back then was full of shallow seas, giant swamps, and impenetrable tropical forests. Dead plants fell into the water—layer upon layer upon layer. Prehistoric sea creatures sank to the bottom of the sea—layer upon layer upon layer. Over the centuries, all the dead junk was covered with a layer of rock. And another layer. And another layer. Those layers squeezed all that stuff together. It got hotter and hotter and started to brew away nicely.

Over millions of years, the remains were pressed together more and more. Where the swamps had been, a thick layer of coal formed, and where the seas had been, oil was created. Vapor rose from the coal and the oil: gas. The gas often went straight into the air. But in some places, there was rock with holes in it and a layer of clay or gypsum on top. The gas was trapped in there for millions of years. Until humans invented the steam engine. And the car. And gas lighting.

FOSSIL ENERGY IS SOLAR ENERGY

Why is there so much energy in oil, gas, and coal? Because it contains plants and animals. That's what you eat when you need energy, isn't it? Have a hamburger, a granola bar, or a glass of apple juice, and you're ready to take on the world again. Animals get energy by eating other animals or plants. And how do plants get energy? Through photosynthesis: they convert sunlight into energy and store it in their leaves and branches. That's why wood burns so well. So, yes: crushed animals and plants are, in fact, stored solar energy.

Guzzling up Energy

Coal was needed to power the steam engine. Oil was needed for cars. And for gas lighting? Um . . . yes, gas was needed. In more and more places, people began taking these fossil fuels from the Earth. All this energy really speeded up the development of the modern world. Machines took the place of craftsmen. Cars replaced horses and carts. People who had once used wood fires now cooked with gas ovens. And power plants allowed almost everyone to get electricity from the outlet whenever they wanted. Most of these power plants still run on coal or gas.

We have since learned that fossil fuels have disadvantages. We believe that they contribute to global warming. And besides, they're going to run out, probably within just a couple centuries. Oil perhaps within about fifty years. I wonder what fuel your car will use then.

FASTER

JUMP iNTO THE ATMOSPHERE

On October 14, 2012, the Austrian daredevil Felix Baumgartner climbed into a capsule under a special air balloon, which took him almost twenty-four miles high. That's four times higher than most airplanes go. That was pretty brave of him. It was even braver when he got out at the highest point and fell back to Earth at a speed of over 844 miles an hour. It's a good thing he remembered to take his parachute . . .

Thin Air

During his stunt, Felix wore a special suit. He needed to, because on the way, he encountered temperatures of around -70 degrees. There was also nowhere near enough oxygen to breathe, and he had no protection from the rays of the sun. In short, at that height, you really don't feel the benefits of the atmosphere. That's because most of the air particles in the atmosphere hang out close to the Earth, because that's where gravity is strongest.[1]

SPACE
(NO ATMOSPHERE)

MORE ATMOSPHERE

ATMOSPHERE

STRATOSPHERE
(6.2/31 MILES)

--- OZONE ---

TROPOSPHERE
(0/6.2 MILES)

At the height where Felix got out of his capsule, the air is very thin: there are far fewer particles in the air. That's why he was able to reach such an incredible speed. An ordinary parachutist who jumps out of a plane at the height of a mile or two is attracted by the Earth's gravity and slowed by the particles in the air. But at first Felix encountered very few particles. So, he went faster and faster, until he got closer to the Earth and found more and more air particles in his way. That's where the gravity of the Earth is strongest, and so the atmosphere is thickest. The particles slowed Felix down, and his parachute did the rest of the work.

AIR PARTICLES?

Air particles, yes. Or would you rather talk about molecules, electrons, and binding? About N_2, O_2, Ar, and CO_2? That's probably not going to make you happy—and it certainly won't make me happy. So take it from me that there are all kinds of tiny little gas particles in the air. If you don't believe it, you just need to go ride your bike fast down a long road. Even when there's no wind, you'll still feel the air streaming past your cheeks. That's all the little air particles that you're cycling into.

Floor Heating

The suit that Felix Baumgartner wore also protected him against the cold. But why is it so much colder at that height? You're closer to the sun, aren't you? Well, mountain summits are closer to the sun than the valleys too. But there's often snow on the mountaintops and not in the valleys.

In the bottom six miles of the atmosphere, it becomes around seventeen degrees (6 degrees Celsius) colder per mile. So, at the top of Mount Everest, it can easily be under -40. This is because most of the heat comes from below and not from above.[2]

The sun's rays hit the Earth full of energy. Some of those rays are reflected back by the atmosphere. The rays that make it through the atmosphere only provide heat when they touch an object. Your skin, for example, or water. Or the hot sandy beach you run across in your bare feet. So the sun warms the Earth, and the Earth warms the air. That's why it's warmer closer to the Earth than at a great height.

Between Earth and Space

Space begins where the atmosphere stops. Lots of newspapers and TV shows called Felix Baumgartner's stunt a space jump, but that's a bit of an exaggeration. There is no clear line between the atmosphere and space. Some people say that space begins at roughly 62 miles (100 kilometers) height. That's why the ISS, which orbits at 248.5 miles (400 kilometers), is called a space station and its inhabitants are astronauts. But others say that space does not begin until 6,213 miles (10,000 kilometers) above our heads.[3] You won't find any of the gas particles that make up our atmosphere out there. The height that Felix reached is in one of the bottom layers of the atmosphere: the stratosphere. That's where he achieved his top speed. One layer below that is the troposphere. He immediately noticed when he reached that layer because the air is much thicker, and so the large numbers of air particles slowed him down.

And Now the Weather

The troposphere is the lowest layer of the atmosphere. This is where by far the most air particles hang out. The air consists of 78 percent nitrogen and 21 percent oxygen. The last bit is made up of other substances, like the famous carbon dioxide (CO_2).[4]

When you watch or read a weather forecast, it's always about the troposphere. Clouds, wind, rain . . . it all happens in the troposphere. The particles in this layer are always on the move. If there are lots of them together, you have a high-pressure area. If there aren't many, you have a low-pressure area. As there is more space in the low-pressure areas, the particles from the high-pressure area flow toward them. We experience that as wind. The same happens when you empty a balloon: the particles inside the balloon are much closer together than the ones outside. The air inside the balloon forms a high-pressure area, and so as soon as they get a chance the particles flow out to the surrounding low-pressure area. You can almost hear them sighing with relief.

Beavers and Scorpions

The weather has everything to do with movements in the troposphere. And those movements depend on differences in temperature and humidity, of the land or water below, and of the location on Earth. That's why it's generally quite a bit hotter in Timbuktu than in Maine and why it rains much more often there than in Timbuktu.

Timbuktu has a different climate than Maine. You can tell that not just by the temperature and the rainfall, but also by the plants that grow there and the animals that live there. You won't see any beavers in Timbuktu or scorpions in Maine. It's time for a little tour. Will you join me?

FROM RAINFOREST TO POLAR CIRCLE

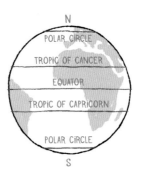

This fantastic route takes you from the equator to the North Pole. From the hot and humid rainforest, you'll travel more than 6,000 miles to the cold, dry polar landscape. Along the way, you'll see the landscape change dramatically. From giant palms, you'll travel to modest lichens: from herds of elephants to solitary polar bears.

The Rainforest of Congo 86°

We begin our route in the Democratic Republic of Congo. This country is exactly halfway up the Earth, on the equator. The equator is just a line on a map, but you can point it out approximately on a satellite photograph too. Nearly all the land around the equator is covered with lush, dark-green forests. Above these areas, you constantly see storms developing. That's because the sun is always so high here. So it quickly becomes warm, the hot air rises, the moisture in the air cools and falls back down as rain.

Because of the humidity and the heat, many, many varieties of plants grow around the equator. The plants attract all kinds of animals, such as gorillas, forest elephants, hornbills, and the amazing okapi, which looks like a mix between a giraffe and a zebra. Nowhere else will you come across as many

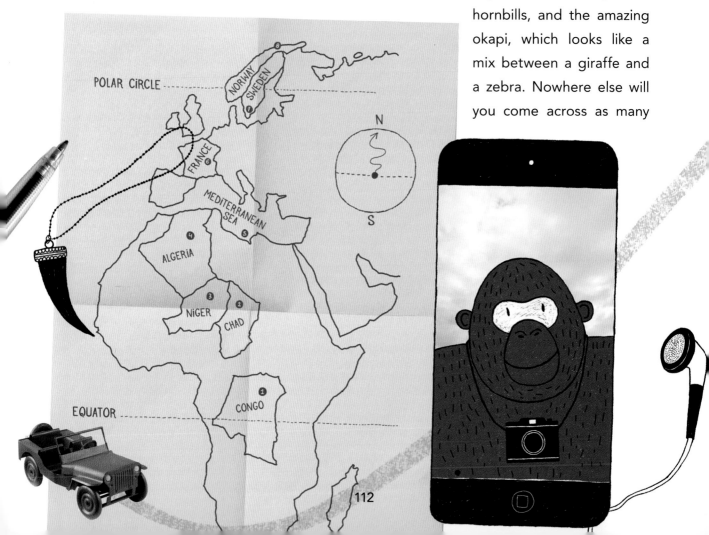

112

THE CONGO'S OKAPI

different species of plants and animals as in the rainforest. We still don't even know how many species coexist there.

The Savanna of Chad 93°

From Congo, we head north. Slowly we see the tropical vegetation disappear. We stop in Chad to take a look at the vast savanna landscape. Savannas can be found all over the world, a little to the north and south of the equator. These areas have two seasons: a wet time when the sun is high and a dry time when the sun is a little lower. The annually recurring drought means that far fewer plants and trees grow here than around the equator. Most of the savanna is covered with grasses, interspersed with clumps of trees and bushes. This attracts grazing animals like gnus, buffalo, zebras, and antelopes. These animals, in turn, attract predators, such as lions, leopards, and hyenas. And all those animals combined attract rich people in Jeeps with their expensive cameras and telephones who want to come and see them.

RATTLING CHAINSAWS

Humans cut down a lot of trees in the tropical rainforests. They do this for the wood itself but also to create land for farming, where they grow crops that we can eat or use for fuel instead of gasoline. Felling the trees does have disadvantages, though. Burning trees releases a lot of CO_2. And when trees disappear, more and more fertile ground gets washed away, and the habitats of animals and plants disappear. They might include some unknown plant that could help to treat cancer or other diseases.

ACACIA TREES IN SAVANNA

The Steppe of Niger 97°

As we travel on, the last vegetation disappears. Not enough rain falls here to feed the trees. Only grass can survive, but for most of the year, it's yellow. When the rain finally falls, the grass turns green and plants suddenly appear everywhere. Welcome to the steppe of Niger.

The steppe is the transition to the desert. You won't find many houses or villages here because the infertile soil is useless for agriculture. So we'll sleep with the Bedouins. Bedouins are nomads: people without a fixed home. Looking for fresh and juicy grass, they move with their livestock from place to place and spend the night in big tents.

A tip from your travel guide: stock up on water at Lake Chad. There are still miles and miles of sand and stone ahead of you, so you'll need it. But don't take more than you require, because Lake Chad is shrinking, and the local people really need the fresh water.

The Desert of Algeria 106°

You might have thought the steppe was dry and hot. Then you should try the Sahara, the biggest sand desert on Earth. The Sahara is made up mostly of sand and rocks. Hardly any plants grow there, because rain almost never falls.

Most deserts are located near the two tropics. These are the places where the sun is directly overhead at the start of summer in June (in the north) and in December (in the south). The weather here comes mostly from the equator. By the time the air arrives at the tropics, there's not a drop of water left in it, because the clouds completely empty themselves above the rainforests.

In the daytime, the temperature in the desert can rise to more than 120 degrees. Then you'll hardly see any animals at all. After sunset, it quickly cools, with some places even reaching temperatures below freezing point. Then you'll see that there are all kinds of creatures living there: gerbils, desert foxes, hyenas, snakes, scorpions, and beetles, for example. The few plants there have long roots to fetch water from deep under the ground and small, thick leaves to prevent evaporation. As little grows there, the wind has free rein in the desert. This allows it to create dunes that are hundreds of feet high and rocks with peculiar shapes.

The Coast of the Mediterranean Sea 80°

Close to the sea, the landscape becomes greener again. Palm trees and olive trees appear in Tunisia, Morocco, Spain, Italy, and the south of France. In the summer, it hardly rains, and the presence of the sea ensures that it's not so cold there in the winter. This is because the sea-water cools down and warms up much more slowly than the land. A lot of elderly people head this way for the winter. The climate here is known as a Mediterranean climate, but it also occurs in other areas by the sea, such as California, South Africa, and Australia.

The Deciduous Forests of France 72°

Now we're diving into the forests of France. Among the trees live various mammals, such as deer, foxes, and wild boar, and birds like woodpeckers, finches, and owls. In this part of Europe, you will find deciduous forests everywhere, although there used to be far more. People felled entire forests to build houses and to make room for cities and fields. By deciduous forests, we mean that the trees here have leaves that fall. They had leaves in the rainforests too, you might say. That's true, but what makes this forest different is the fact that the leaves fall. And this is all to do with the big differences between the seasons, this far from the equator.

The trees lose most water through their leaves. By shedding their leaves in the fall, the trees protect themselves from the cold of the winter. Water often freezes in the wintertime, and the trees would dry out if they still had leaves. By the time the frosts are over, new leaves are growing on the trees. From springtime, there is enough water again for the leaves to let it evaporate.

The Coniferous Forests of Sweden 57°

We're heading farther north, and so it's getting colder again. The Earth is at a bit of angle, so the days and nights can last a very long time here. In the summer, it stays light for a long time; in the winter, it's dark for a long time. The sun is never high in the sky here, so it's a bit too cold for deciduous trees. Coniferous trees take their place. These trees have needles, which have a much smaller surface area than a leaf. This means that they receive less sunlight and evaporate much less water. And so a coniferous tree can survive in places where a deciduous tree would never last. But let's be honest—a needle is in fact the same as a leaf. It's just rolled up tightly.

Fewer plants grow in coniferous forests than in more southern forests. The trees are closer together and let through less sunlight. And also, no leaves fall that could make humus, the rotting stuff that makes the soil so nice and fertile. Some small plants that do enjoy living in coniferous forests are mosses. They're not usually too fussy about the ground they live on. Animals you might encounter here are the moose, the wolf, and the brown bear.

The Tundra of Norway 18°

By now, it's about seventy degrees colder than when we left Congo. But don't worry—we're nearly there. Now we're traveling to the North Cape in Norway. We've reached the tundra. The tundra covers just about the entire northern coast of Europe, Asia, and America. It's like a ring around the North Pole.

There are no trees to be found in the tundra. All that can grow here is grass, moss, and a few little bushes. More than half of the year, the soil here is frozen. The other half of the year, just a small part of the ground beneath our feet thaws. As the soil is frozen, it is hard for the water to drain away. And there is not much sun to make it evaporate either. So the tundra is pretty marshy. Don't forget your rubber boots.

We are above the polar circle. That means that in the summer, there are days when it doesn't get dark, and there are days in the winter when it doesn't get light. If you travel on to the North Pole, you'll notice the days there last about six months, and so does the night.

At the North Pole, almost as little precipitation falls as in the Sahara. But it's much colder around the North Pole, so little water evaporates and there's a lot of snow and ice. The grass and the last few bushes can't cope here either. Only some mosses survive the minimum temperatures of -75 degrees.

It is just one big desert of ice and snow. Animals who feel at home here include polar bears, arctic foxes, and walruses.

Have a Good Trip Home!

We have reached the end of our tour. We hope you enjoyed it. To get back home, you can travel across the North Pole and then head back down south. You'll pass through different countries, but you'll experience more or less the same climates and landscapes.

It'll slowly become warmer again. The grasses and plants will reappear. Then the conifers and the deciduous trees. Around the tropics, it'll be bare again, and dry, and hot. After that, you'll see wide plains full of animals, and when you get stuck in the tropical plants, you'll know that the equator can't be too far off.

pole pole pole
tundra tundra tundra tundra
coniferous coniferous coniferous
deciduous deciduous deciduous deciduous
desert desert desert desert desert desert desert
steppe steppe steppe steppe steppe steppe steppe
savanna savanna savanna savanna savanna savanna savanna
rainforest rainforest rainforest rainforest rainforest rainforest
savanna savanna savanna savanna savanna savanna savanna
steppe steppe steppe steppe steppe steppe steppe
desert desert desert desert desert desert desert
deciduous deciduous deciduous deciduous
coniferous coniferous coniferous
tundra tundra tundra tundra
pole pole pole

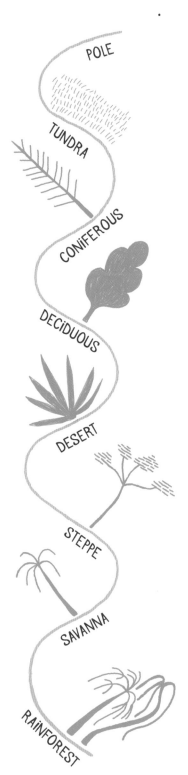

POLE

TUNDRA

CONIFEROUS

DECIDUOUS

DESERT

STEPPE

SAVANNA

RAINFOREST

THERE'S A QUICKER WAY

In Mérida, Venezuela, you'll find an incredible cable car ride. At the ground station, it's still hot and humid. On the way up, you'll see the trees and plants of the rainforest slowly disappearing and giving way to succulents and mosses. When you're at the top, you won't see any plants at all, just rocks and snow. So within an hour, you'll have traveled from 85 degrees to 25 degrees—from a tropical climate to a polar one.[5]

WHEN IS THE NEXT ICE AGE?

Around 20,000 years ago, you could walk from Alaska all the way to Russia. That was perfect, because no one had even heard of ferries, airplanes, or train tunnels yet. Anyone making the crossing would have been wise to put on a fur hat and an extra bearskin. It was bitingly cold on the endless plains of ice, and there was a nasty wind because no trees grew there.

Between Mammoth and Cave Lion

Twenty thousand years ago, the last ice age was coming to an end. Much of Europe, North America, and Russia was covered with a thick layer of ice. As there was so much water in the ice, the water in the seas was over 400 feet lower.[6]

So, the North Sea of the Atlantic Ocean was completely dry. For thousands of years, the region alternated between the harsh climates of the polar desert and the steppe. During the slightly warmer periods, grass, plants, and small trees grew there. You could encounter herds of reindeer and woolly mammoths along the way, and you had to take care not to bump into any wolves or cave lions. Fishermen there today regularly bring up mammoth bones and tusks.

Climate Change Is Nothing New

The climate is just like the landscape; it is constantly changing. There have been times when palm trees grew and hippopotamuses and hyenas walked around in the far northern part of the world—species you would now expect to find in tropical Africa. But animals we only see at the North Pole these days also used to live farther south.

Over the past 2.6 million years, there has been an ice age every 100,000 years, on average.[7] It's too bad that prehistoric humans didn't make satellites. Imagine what those

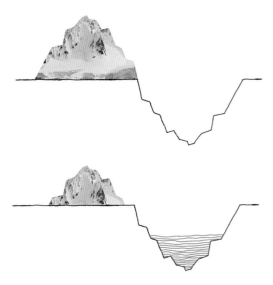

2.6 million years of satellite photographs would look like if you played them really quickly like a film. The ice of the poles would spread toward the equator like a big blob of bird poo, while at the same time, the seas would empty out as if someone had pulled the plug. Then you would see the ice retreating to the poles and the seas filling up again. Then another blob of bird poo and the water draining again. And so on and so on, like a flashing light—but a flashing light that sometimes goes a bit faster and sometimes goes a bit slower.

Ice Ages for Beginners

Ice ages happen when the differences between the seasons on Earth are smaller than usual, when the summers are just a little bit colder and the winters are just a little bit warmer. That gives glaciers more chance to grow. This is how it works: In very cold winters, less rain and snow falls, because less water evaporates.

So slightly warmer winters mean extra snow. That snow gradually changes into thick layers of ice. If the summers are cooler, less of that ice melts, and the glaciers can grow a little more the following winter. That allows the ice to advance slowly to the south. The Earth turns whiter and whiter. And that makes the planet even cooler, because white reflects more sunlight than the dark colors of soil, moss, and trees. That's why you're better off wearing a white T-shirt in the blazing sun than a black one: black absorbs heat, while white reflects it.

This effect of the white ground reflecting the sunlight works mainly in the northern hemisphere. That makes sense, because there is more land there for the glaciers to color white. The ice caps of the North Pole can expand much more easily because they need to cross fewer seas than the ice caps of the South Pole.

But how does an ice age begin, and how does it end? It's all to do with the distance between the Earth and the sun and with the position of the Earth's axis. It's a complicated story, so feel free to skip it.

Ice Ages for Advanced Students

iCE AGE!

MiLUTiN MiLANKOVIĆ
1879 – 1958

About a century ago, a Milutin Milanković from Serbia wondered where ice ages came from and why they had such a strange rhythm. He took a close look at the position of the globe. He noticed three things that, together, can explain the ice ages:

1. The Earth moves in an ellipse around the sun. But that ellipse is rounder at some times than others. The attraction of Jupiter and Saturn changes the distance between the Earth and the sun a little. In 100,000 years, the course changes from an ellipse into almost a circle and back again.

2. The axis of the Earth is more tilted at some times than others. The Earth's axis takes 41,000 years to go from its most tilted position to its straightest position, and back again.

3. The Earth's axis also wobbles a little, a bit like a spinning top. This is because the sun and the moon both pull at our planet. After 26,000 years, the Earth's axis is back to exactly where it was 23,000 years before.[8]

All three of these factors have an influence on the differences between the seasons, particularly when combined. When the Earth's axis is straighter, for example, there is less difference between the seasons and more chance of an ice age. The next ice age is planned for around 25,000 years' time. Why not put it in your planner already?

OF COURSE THE CLIMATE IS CHANGING

People say that the Earth is getting warmer and warmer and that the ice caps are melting. They say that water levels are rising and that dozens of US cities will be flooded within 100 years.[9] They say that the weather is going to be boiling hot, then soaking wet, and then as dry as a bone, more and more often. They say that it's our own fault. But is that true?

A Great Greenhouse

In the atmosphere, there are gases that hold on to some of the sun's heat. They make the Earth into a greenhouse, letting in sunlight but holding on to the warmth that comes back from the Earth. And that is good, because without this greenhouse

effect, the average temperature on Earth would be almost sixty degrees lower than it is now.[10] You can assume that you wouldn't be here. So your life was, in part, made possible by greenhouse gases like water vapor, carbon dioxide (CO_2), methane (CH_4), and laughing gas (N_2O).

Too Much Greenhouse

In recent years, more and more of these greenhouse gases have entered the air. A large group of scientists from all kinds of different countries has spent years researching the greenhouse effect. They have drilled down for miles into the ice of Antarctica to bring up air bubbles that got stuck in the ice thousands of years ago. Their conclusion: over the past 800,000 years, there were not as many greenhouse gases in the atmosphere as there are now.[11] Those gases are holding on to more and more heat. The scientists calculated that it has not been as warm on Earth in a million years as it has in recent years and that in 2100 it could be 5.5 degrees warmer than the planet's 57-degree average we have now. In some places the increase in temperature could be a lot higher.[12]

That heat has meant that a lot of the snow and ice at the poles and in the mountains have melted. Since 1901, sea levels have also risen by around seven inches. This is because of the melting ice but also because warm water needs more space than cold water.[13]

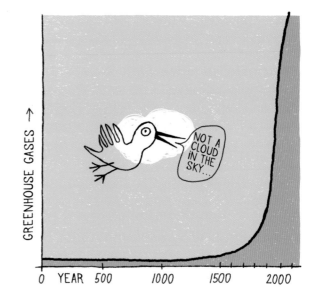

How Did It Happen?

Some people wonder if it was humans who put all those extra greenhouse gases in the air. You might think so. Take a look at this graph showing the amount of greenhouse gases over the centuries. Until around 1800, you see a line quietly bobbing along: the quantities of greenhouse gases in the atmosphere remain almost the same for thousands of years. But from 1800, you see the line suddenly rising steeply as lots and lots of greenhouse gases enter the atmosphere.

What happened around 1800 again? Wasn't there something about an industrial revolution, steam engines, coal? Of course! Around two hundred years ago, people began building factories all over the place. With big chimneys pumping out thick clouds of black smoke. About 100 years later, the car was invented. There are now more than a billion cars driving around on Earth, with exhaust pipes pumping out slightly less thick clouds of smoke.

And those clouds of smoke contain—you guessed it—greenhouse gases.

CO_2 Is Okay

The most important greenhouse gas is carbon dioxide, also known as CO_2. There is not actually much wrong with CO_2 itself. It's in the soda that you drink, in the food you eat, and in the air you breathe out. When the Earth was not very old, there was a lot more CO_2 in the air. This was mainly because of all the volcanic explosions. Plants use CO_2 to grow. With the help of the sunlight, they convert CO_2 into leaves, wood, and roots, and they emit oxygen. As a

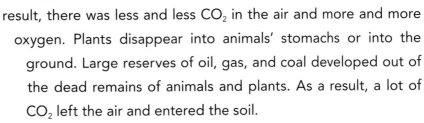

result, there was less and less CO_2 in the air and more and more oxygen. Plants disappear into animals' stomachs or into the ground. Large reserves of oil, gas, and coal developed out of the dead remains of animals and plants. As a result, a lot of CO_2 left the air and entered the soil.

These past few centuries, we've actually been doing the opposite: taking fossil fuels out of the ground and burning them. So, the CO_2 is reentering the air at breakneck speed.

Good evening,
this is the news on Wednesday,
September 8, 2106:

THE NEWS OF THE FUTURE

20:08

INDIA AND BANGLADESH FIGHTING OVER WATER

The dispute between Bangladesh and northeast India is becoming increasingly serious. Soldiers from both sides have gathered at the border. The countries have been in a dispute for years about the course of the River Ganges. Now that most of the glaciers in the Himalayas have melted, little more remains of the once-mighty river than a tiny stream. People in both countries need the water for agriculture and drinking. This is creating huge problems in one of the most densely populated areas of the world.

STORM SURGE BARRIER CLOSED AGAIN

The Storm Barrier in Lower New York Bay was closed once again this morning. For the third time in four years, there is a storm blowing from the southeast with gusts of over 100 miles an hour. The situation is less serious than in April of last year, when the high water levels in the Hudson river made closing the surge barrier risky for the river land. All work to reinforce the barrier and levees has been temporarily suspended.

Add to that the fact that humans have felled a lot of trees to use as raw materials and to make way for cities and agriculture. The CO_2 from those trees has also entered the air.

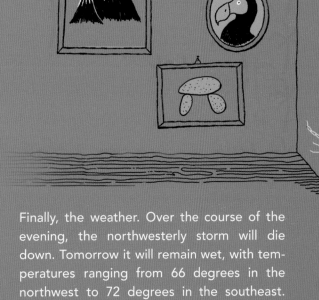

FOOD PRiCES REACH RECORD HiGH

The continuing drought in the Mediterranean has pushed food prices even higher. Disappointing harvests have followed pessimistic reports from Russia, where major agricultural areas have been struggling with extreme rainfall for weeks. Worldwide restrictions on fishing have also been extended, now that it has been established that most species of fish in the former coral zones are only slowly recovering.

RESiDENTS OF TUVALU ARRiVE iN AUSTRALIA

In Australia, the last inhabitants of Tuvalu have arrived. This former paradise in the Pacific Ocean is now completely at the mercy of the sea. Locals have taken their belongings and left their homes as empty as possible. Special houses have been prepared in Sydney and Brisbane to accommodate the displaced Tuvaluans, helped by the experiences of the former inhabitants of the Maldives.

THE FiRST WiLD GECKO iN BELGiUM

In the southeast of Belgium, a gecko has been spotted for the first time. This creature, a species of gecko until recently found only in the south of Europe, is doing very well, according to experts. The gecko could play an important role in the fight against malaria, now that the malaria mosquito also appears to have found its way to the north.

Finally, the weather. Over the course of the evening, the northwesterly storm will die down. Tomorrow it will remain wet, with temperatures ranging from 66 degrees in the northwest to 72 degrees in the southeast. The next few days will gradually become drier and the temperature should rise. We'll close tonight with pictures from New York, where Hurricane Zelda has just flooded the center of Manhattan.

And that's the news for this evening. I wish you all a good night.

What Are We Going to Do About It?

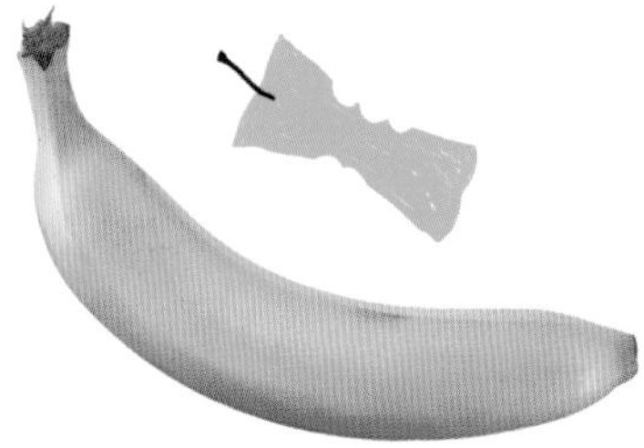

The Earth is becoming warmer and warmer. Even if we close all the factories down today and abandon all our cars, this warming will continue for centuries. So what can we do? We can adapt to the new situation and emit fewer greenhouse gases.

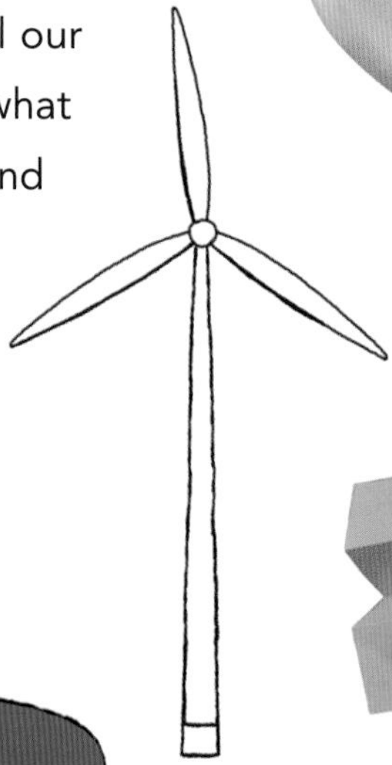

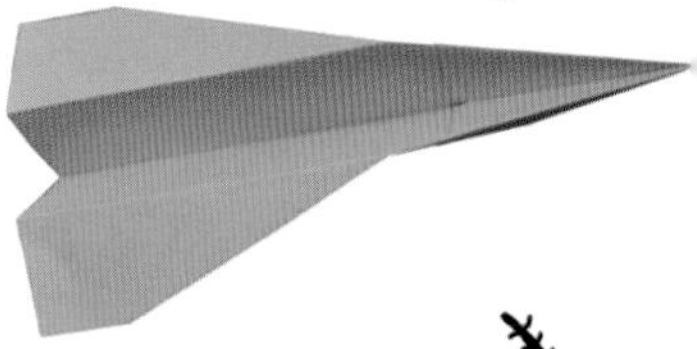

Adapting means, for example, creating better flood defenses in low-lying areas, preparing for refugees from regions with drought or floods, and cultivating crops that need less— or more—water.

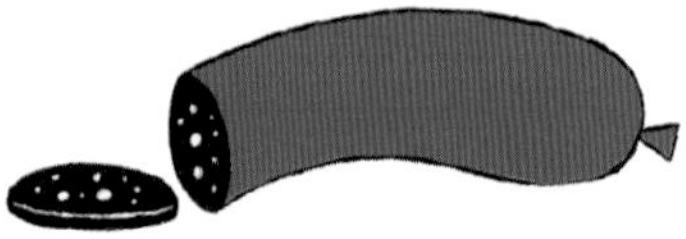

Meanwhile, we can try to send less CO_2 into the air. The problem is that more and more people keep coming along who, like the rest of us, want a car, an iPad, a vacation by plane . . . So, we can build windmill parks and solar power stations, but new coal plants will still be built because we need more energy. An additional problem is that countries need to tackle climate change together, as it's an issue that affects the whole world. So there are lots of meetings and not many decisions. Luckily, there are some things you can do yourself.

HIGHLY FLAMMABLE
NO MORE
FOSSILS

SAFETY MATCHES

PURE NATURE

FIVE TIPS

1. Go on vacation by plane as little as possible. Planes emit the most CO_2 per passenger.[14]

2. Eat less meat. A cow emits as much greenhouse gas in a day as you driving around in a car all day. That's a lot of methane![15]

3. Don't use fossil fuels. Go for wind energy or solar power, instead of coal or gas.

4. Buy local products. Eat fruits and vegetables that are grown around your town or even in your home state, which use less energy (and emit less CO_2) than those being grown and flown or trucked in from thousands of miles away (like in Central and South America). The transport of produce from distant lands is the main culprit of high-carbon-footprint products. Also fruits and vegetables grown outside use the power of the sun and possibly even get some water from rain, meaning they use less energy than those cultivated in greenhouses.

5. Use your bike instead of the car.

HOW TO SURVIVE EXTREME WEATHER

How do you think that spider felt when you washed it down the drain the other day? And those ants you casually vacuumed up? The wood lice in the piece of wood you threw onto the fire? Powerless, probably, if they felt anything at all. Powerless, and overwhelmed, and tiny. Like a person in a flood, a hurricane, or a forest fire.

How Hurricanes Happen

Hurricanes develop at the end of the summer in the tropics, just above and below the equator. Then the seawater's so warm that lots and lots of water evaporates at once. The damp air rises and cools, creating a low-pressure area with dense storm clouds. The wind and the rotation of the Earth make the clouds start turning. As long as the hurricane is over the sea, it can keep growing. The warm water feeds the hurricane. When it hits land, it quickly loses strength—there's no more water left to evaporate then.

A hurricane is the same thing as a typhoon. The difference is that hurricanes happen around America, and typhoons are in Asia. Hurricanes are particularly dangerous because of the tidal waves they can cause. If the land is low, the water can travel for miles. The wind

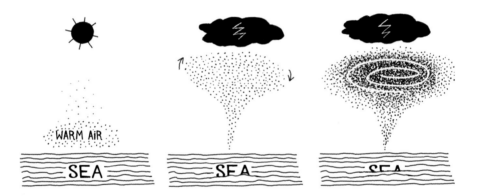

and rain cause problems too. In 2017, Hurricane Harvey hit Southeast Texas and holds the record for the highest rainfall ever with a total of 60.58 inches. Compare that to the wettest state, Hawaii, which averages 70.3 inches of rain in a year! That is one wet storm.[16]

How to Survive a Hurricane

- Nail windows shut and secure loose objects.
- Fill the bathtub and buckets with drinking water for after the hurricane.
- Charge all of your devices for as long as you can.

- Go sit in the basement or under the stairs. If you can't do that, lie under a mattress.
- If there is no sturdy building, a cave is the best place to hide. There's no cave nearby? Then go look for a ditch and lie in it, flat on the ground.
- Stay away from the sea and riverbank. Keep away from trees, fences, and other things that might fall over.
- When the wind dies down, stay where you are. At the center (the eye) of the hurricane, there is no wind, but the second half of the hurricane will probably come along within thirty minutes or so.

How Tornados Happen

A tornado is much smaller than a hurricane and usually lasts no longer than a few minutes. However, the wind speed in a tornado can get up to more than 300 miles an hour.[17] Tornados develop during fierce storms, when the air on the ground is much warmer than the higher air. The warm air rises so quickly that a small low-pressure area develops on the ground, which sucks all the air toward it. A twisting tube develops, as a twisting movement is the fastest way to move; that's also why water twists down the drain. Tornados happen mainly in the United States and Australia. Another word for "tornado" is a cyclone. Whirlwinds and waterspouts occur in other parts of the world. They develop in the same way as tornados, but they're much weaker and less dangerous.

How to Survive a Tornado

- Don't try to run ahead of a tornado.
- Find shelter in the basement of a sturdy building, away from windows and objects that can fall.

- No basement? Then hide in the middle of the bottom floor under a strong table or sofa, but make sure there's nothing heavy directly over you on the floor above you. Avoid windows and cover your head, even with your arms.

- If you cannot safely leave your car during a tornado, park out of traffic, keep your seat belt on, get lower than the windows, and cover your head.

- What if you can't get to shelter? Go lie in a ditch, with your arms over your head.

How Landslides Happen

A landslide is different from an earthquake. An earthquake comes from inside the Earth, but with a landslide, a slope suddenly collapses. It usually happens after heavy rainstorms turn the soil into mud. On a steep slope, the whole thing can come sliding down. It's often poor people who suffer. They want to live close to the city but have to make do with places that aren't really suitable for construction, such as steep slopes. Some time ago, 30,000 people were swallowed by a river of mud in Venezuela.[18] Felling trees on the mountains causes problems too, as tree roots help to keep the soil together.

How to Survive a Landslide

- Avoid steep slopes during extreme rainfall.

- Is there a risk of landslides? Find shelter in a sturdy building.

- Head to higher floors if you can, because mudflows are likely not to reach you there.

How Floods Happen

Seawater floods come about mainly because of tidal waves in a storm or after an earthquake. Rivers and streams overflow when a lot of rain falls or if snow melts in the area the river is coming from. People who live near the Columbia River and the Rhine know all about that, but the water that flows through those rivers is peanuts in comparison to the Mekong and the Ganges in southern Asia. There you can just sit waiting for the flood, as it happens around the same time every year. This is because of the monsoon, a wind that blows from the sea to the land half of the year, and from the land to the sea the other half of the year. This is all to do with low-pressure areas: In the summer, the land warms up more quickly than the

sea. A low-pressure area develops over the land then. The wet air from the sea blows that way, rises, cools, and forms rain. In the winter the situation is reversed; then the drier air blows from the land to the sea.

How to Survive a Flood

- Don't let a flood take you by surprise. Aim to be on a hill, not in a valley.

- If there's a risk of flooding, make your way to higher ground.

- Take precautions if there's a flood risk: find a sturdy, multifloor building and on the top floor, create a stock of drinking water, food, rope, blankets, a flashlight, a radio, and extra batteries.

- Turn off the gas and electricity and go to the top floor of the building. If the water rises so high that you have to sit on the roof, make sure everyone is tied to something strong.

- If the water looks like it's going to rise higher than the roof, build a raft.

- Try to alert rescue workers with your flashlight.

How Droughts Happen

Droughts happen when it doesn't rain much and when a lot of water evaporates. In deserts, in other words. But droughts can suddenly occur in other places too, for example, when a high-pressure area sends the normal storms and showers in another direction. In many countries, they find themselves longing for rain every year.

Humans are also a cause of drought. By felling trees, they allow the wind to blow freely and the desert to expand. By using water for agriculture, swimming pools, and golf courses, they lower water levels in lakes and in the soil. This means that, in some places, it's difficult to get hold of clean water, and there's also a shortage of food.

How to Survive a Drought

- Try to prevent drought by being careful with water.

- Prepare by stocking up on water and protecting it from evaporation.

- Don't move too much, and avoid the sun.

- Boil all water before you drink it in case it has been contaminated.

- Even if there is not much water, wash your hands after using the bathroom and before preparing food. Sickness could be a greater threat than thirst.

- Reuse water. Water that you've used for cooking is still good for washing yourself.

How Forest Fires Happen

There's nothing unusual about a forest fire. The United States alone has around 100,000 each year.[19] They usually happen in extreme drought and heat. Just one little spark can be enough to start a forest fire. For example, when walkers are careless with cigarettes or when lighting a fire. Sometimes people deliberately set woodland on fire. They probably get a kick out of the attention they receive in the news but are shocked by the consequences. Forest fires happened even before there were people around, though. Back then, it was lightning that sparked the fire. Many forests bounce back after a fire and are surprisingly strong: the ash from the dead wood makes the soil fertile, and young plants and trees soon occupy the open spaces.

How to Survive a Forest Fire

- Be very careful in woodland during droughts. Make sure you don't cause any fires yourself and that you can escape if a fire starts.

- Don't just run. Think first which way the fire is heading.

- Run into the wind and downhill, unless that's where the fire is. Fire moves faster uphill than downhill.

- Try to reach an open space: a lake, a river, a ravine, or some other place where there are no trees and bushes.

- Wait in water until the fire is over. Breathe through a wet cloth to protect your lungs.

- Isn't there any water nearby? Then lie in a dip or a ditch and cover your body with sand or wet clothes. Good luck!

EL NIÑO

Once every few years the weather changes completely. On the west coast of South America, it is warm and rains much more than normal, even in the deserts. At the same time, in Australia and Indonesia, it is cooler and much drier, even in the rainforests. The extra rain causes landslides and the drought results in big forest fires.

El Niño (pronounced: El Neen-yo) happens when the water of the Pacific Ocean between South America and Indonesia is warmer than usual for a long time. The wind and the current of the water change, with serious consequences. Not just for the weather, but also for nature. There are fewer nutrients in the warm water, and that means fewer fish in the sea. The fishermen in Peru noticed that it often happens around Christmas and so called the phenomenon El Niño, Spanish for "Little Boy" but also often used to mean "Christ child."[20]

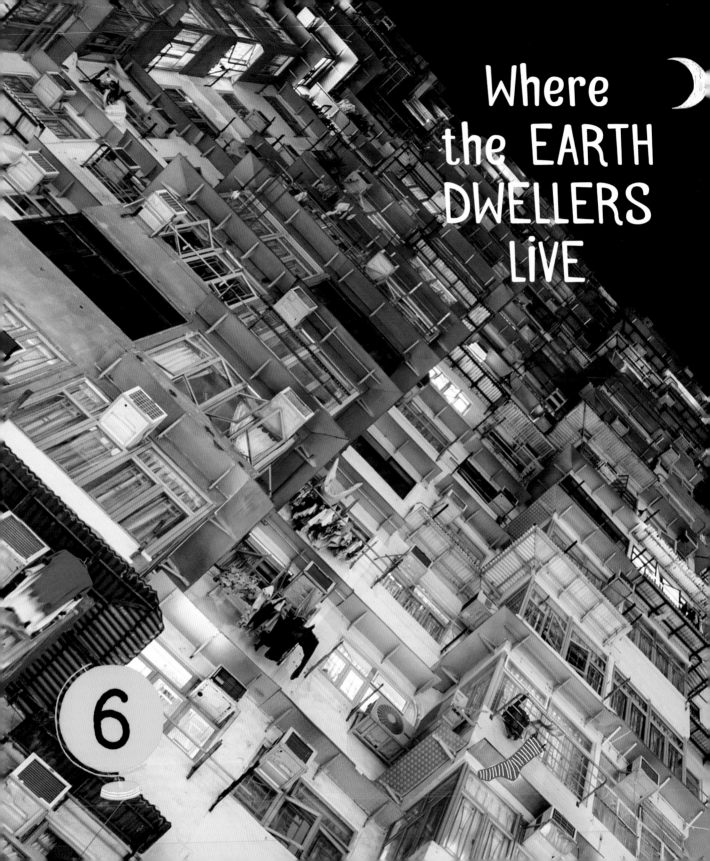

Where the EARTH DWELLERS LIVE

6

THE FIRST PEOPLE

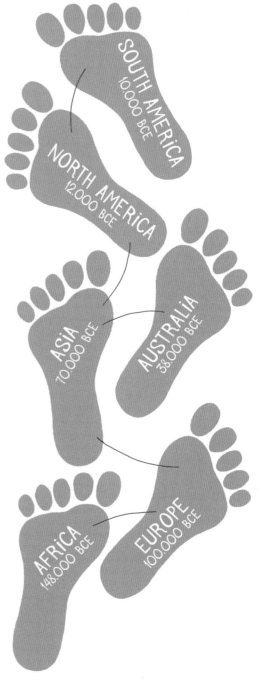

Let's go back in time—150,000 years, just a blink in the history of the Earth. No one knows yet that the Earth is round. No one has ever seen a satellite photo of our planet. And no one needs to remember that Madison is the capital of Wisconsin.

Save Your Tribe

You know the area where your tribe lives like the back of your hand, but there is no world for you beyond that. All you know is that the sun always rises above the sea and sets behind the mountains. You know that three days' walk with your shadow at your back takes you to the deer plain, the plain where there are no deer right now. So, for many moons, you've been living on the fruit from the woods on the hill. But they're almost gone now too. The head of your tribe has told you that beyond the mountains is a river no one has ever crossed. The drought means that the water is probably lower than usual. Maybe you could make it across. You have no choice: you have to give it a try because the tribe is hungry. So you set off with three of the strongest members of the tribe. You don't have a GPS with you and no map of the surroundings. There are no roads and no helpful signs to show you the way: *FERTILE VALLEY 23 MILES*. You don't know what kind of animals you'll meet along the way: slow lizards that you can catch and munch on, or wild hyenas who are just as hungry as you. You look back one last time at your tribe and see how thin they are. All their hopes are pinned on you.

Out into the Wide World

This was how the first humans set out. Looking for food, looking for space, escaping from drought. As hunter-gatherers, they always roamed the same area, but sometimes circumstances forced them to look further afield. Then a whole tribe, or just some of them, would leave their familiar territory to avoid overpopulation.

The first modern people lived in Africa around 150,000 years ago. Some of them slowly spread out around the world. They followed rivers and coastlines and eventually reached Europe and Asia. They had to build good ships before they were able to get to Australia too, around 40,000 years ago. North America probably remained uninhabited for a long time. In the last ice age, the sea between Asia and America dried out, and people were able to make the crossing. For over 2,000 years, successive waves of people moved across the land bridge from Siberia and slowly made their way from the north of North America to the south of South America.[1] This was about 12,000 years ago. Human beings had populated every continent, except for Antarctica. Estimates say that there were around 3 million people in the world at that moment,[2] the same number as now live in the city of Berlin.

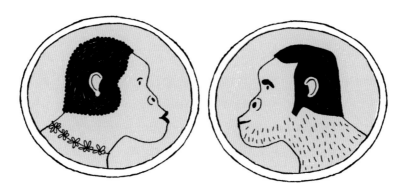

Your Ancestors

Those 3 million people included the grandma of the
grandma of the grandma of the grandma of the grandma of the grandma
of the grandma of the grandma of the grandma of the grandma of the grandma of
the grandma of the grandma of the grandma of the grandma of the grandma of the grandma
of the grandma of the grandma of the grandma of the grandma of the grandma of the grandma of the
grandma of the grandma of the grandma of the grandma of the grandma of the grandma of the grandma
of the grandma of the grandma of the grandma of the grandma of the grandma of the grandma of the grandma
of the grandma of the grandma of the grandma of the grandma of the grandma of the grandma of the grandma of the
grandma of the grandma of the grandma of the grandma of the grandma of the grandma of the grandma of the grandma
of the grandma of the grandma of the grandma of the grandma of the grandma (champion berry picker!) of the grandma of
the grandma of the grandma of the grandma of the grandma of the grandma of the grandma of the grandma of the grandma of
the grandma of the grandma of the grandma of the grandma of the grandma of the grandma of the grandma of the grandma of the
grandma of the grandma of the grandma of the grandma of the grandma of the grandma of the grandma of the grandma of the grandma
of the grandma of the grandma of the grandma of the grandma of the grandma of the grandma of the grandma of the grandma of the
grandma of the grandma of the grandma of the grandma of the grandma of the grandma of the grandma of the grandma of the grandma of
the grandma of the grandma of the grandma of the grandma of the grandma of the grandma of the grandma of the grandma of the grandma of
the grandma of the grandma of the grandma of the grandma of the grandma of the grandma of the grandma of the grandma of the grandma of
the grandma of the grandma of the grandma of the grandma of the grandma of the grandma of the grandma of the grandma of the grandma of
the grandma of the grandma of the grandma of the grandma of the grandma of the grandma of the grandma of the grandma of the grandma of
the grandma of the grandma of the grandma of the grandma of the grandma of the grandma (a famous potter among the builders of megalithic
tombs) of the grandma of the grandma of the grandma of the grandma of the grandma of the grandma of the grandma of the grandma of the
grandma of the grandma of the grandma of the grandma of the grandma of the grandma of the grandma of the grandma of the grandma of the grandma
of the grandma of the grandma of the grandma of the grandma of the grandma of the grandma of the grandma of the grandma of the grandma of the
grandma of the grandma of the grandma of the grandma of the grandma of the grandma of the grandma of the grandma of the grandma of the grandma
of the grandma of the grandma of the grandma of the grandma of the grandma of the grandma of the grandma of the grandma of the grandma of
the grandma of the grandma of the grandma of the grandma of the grandma of the grandma of the grandma of the grandma of the grandma of
the grandma of the grandma of the grandma of the grandma of the grandma of the grandma of the grandma of the grandma of the grandma
of the grandma of the grandma of the grandma of the grandma of the grandma of the grandma of the grandma of the grandma of the
grandma of the grandma of the grandma of the grandma of the grandma of the grandma of the grandma of the grandma of the
grandma of the grandma of the grandma of the grandma (who had her portrait painted by the famous Han Gan
of China) of the grandma of the grandma of the grandma of the grandma of the grandma of the grandma
of the grandma of the grandma of the grandma of the grandma of the grandma of the grandma of the grandma
of the grandma of the grandma of the grandma (the Franklins' next-door neighbor when
little Benjamin was born) of the grandma of the grandma of the grandma of the
grandma of the grandma of the grandma of the grandma of your
grandma. And of your grandpa, of course. Do you think
you look like them?

Eat Local

We know your ancestors didn't buy their food at the supermarket on the corner. But where did they get their food from? Did they stick with being hunter-gatherers for generations, or did they transition quickly to be farmers? Maybe they did a bit of both. Around 10,000 years ago was the time when the benefits of agriculture were discovered in various places in the world. People started to keep animals, which gave them milk, eggs, and meat. They began to cultivate grain, so that they wouldn't have to look so hard for food. Agriculture was a worldwide hit. More food for less effort. People became better and better at farming, and they kept the best seeds to plant their new crop. Increasingly often, there was even food left over. This had major consequences.

WORLD TRADE MARKET

GOLD

As it became easier to get hold of food, more children were born and people lived longer. The world's population started growing unstoppably. They also had time to do other things than searching for food. People began to make tools, pottery, weapons, ships. They went out in those ships to explore the world.

After humans had spent 140,000 years spreading out all over the world, now they began visiting one another. Not because they'd been missing one another, because they didn't even know that all those other people existed. No, they went to look for raw materials that they didn't have themselves: dyes, oil, herbs, exotic fruits. The time of trade and exploration had begun.

GUESS THE WORLD MAAAAP!

Hello and welcome to *Guess the World Maaaap!*—the quiz in which contestants from all kinds of different eras and countries try to fill in an almost blank world map.

> **Note from the publisher:** Some of these "contestants" were in many ways conquerors first, explorers second. Often their mission was to uncover natural resources to take back to their countries—at the expense of the native peoples they encountered along the way. These conquerors didn't really care about the well-being of the people they met on their trips and sometimes were the cause of great suffering and pain.

Here's a quick reminder of the rules:

1. All the contestants have to start in their own country.
2. Contestants can make use of all the means of transport they have at their disposal.
3. Points are scored for every region that contestants put on the map.

Egyptians, Polynesians, the Netherlands, the Vikings, and everyone else . . . are you ready to play? Let's see the first world map!

10,000 BCE

Wow, that big, blank world map really is very empty indeed. We can see a whole bunch of dots spread out across the world, though. Those must be our contestants. They have no idea about the world around them. Which makes sense. After all, it's 10,000 years ago! Ah, but look, a small bit of coastline is appearing. Ahh, those poor Phoenicians don't dare to go out onto the open sea yet. Wait a second, now I can see a bit of the Mediterranean emerging. Hey, look, and there's someone sailing along the Nile. That must be the Egyptians! Now we can see more and more islands becoming visible in the southeast of the map. How brave of our Polynesian friends in their boats!

Fourth Century BCE

Hey, so now we've got a whole lot of coastlines, guys! Why don't you try going inland? Look, Alexander the Great is really going for it: he's taking his own mapmakers with him on his expedition. Aha, and now we can see a bit more of Greece, Egypt, and India. Way to go, Alexander!

144

PHOENICIANS

EGYPTIANS

ALEXANDER
the GREAT

MARCO POLO

VIKINGS

WILLEM
BARENTSZ

CHRISTOPHER
COLUMBUS

FERDINAND
MAGELLAN

VASCO da
GAMA

JAMES COOK

ABEL TASMAN

WILLEM
JANSZOON

First Century

Now, for Rome, we have the gentleman Pliny the Elder. Oh, and he thinks he's just going to describe half the world. Now we can see Africa, Asia, and southern Europe becoming clearer and clearer. But no, Mr. Pliny, there are no one-legged creatures living in India with a foot that they use as a parasol. Hey, that's not going to earn you any bonus points. But those camel-like animals with spots like a leopard and a long, long neck? Yep, they're approved, and so are the big gray animals with enormous ears and a long snake-like thing instead of a nose. The rest of the contestants are looking skeptical, but no: they really do exist!

Second Century

I just received a bet from a Greek map-maker called Ptolemy. He says that in the south of the map, there's some kind of fantastic continent. Well, we'll see about that, Mr. Ptolemy. That still needs to be proven. How about we call it Terra Incognita for now—Unknown Land?

Ninth Century

Finally, there's some movement in the north. Must be the Vikings. Wow, half the coastline of Europe is suddenly there. Oh, and just to make it clear: All you have to do is put the place on the map, right? There's no need for looting. Hey, look at that, they've gone for a chunk of America. Oh, now that's caused some grumpy faces in the Spanish camp.

Thirteenth Century

Take a look at Italy now, because Marco Polo's just setting off with his retinue, heading straight for China. We can see

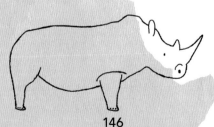

146

more and more details of Turkey, Iran, India, China. And he's going over the sea and across the land. You see, guys, that's an option too! Now, look, the Arabs are going into the Sahara and to the mountains of India. And, like it's just a piece of cake, they're sailing off to eastern Africa, China, and Indonesia. So what do we have now? Part of Africa, Europe, Asia, and a little bit of America and Greenland. But yeah, the edges of the map are still completely blank, and we're almost in the fifteenth century. Do you think there's some great big sea all around or something?

Fifteenth Century

I shouldn't have said that. Now Portugal's getting involved. Here we go—suddenly we can see the entire coastline of Africa. Spain has decided to put an Italian into the game: Christopher Columbus. And why not? There he goes, sailing west to find a quick route to Asia. But, Columbus, America is in the way! Columbus insists that he has found the Indies, and so he calls the inhabitants Indians. *Please take care with the Indians*, they added. But oh no: Columbus doesn't listen.

Meanwhile, in the east, it's a madhouse. Madagascar has been added, and the interior of Indonesia. Thank you, Vasco da Gama! Ferdinand Magellan's ship is the first to sail around the world. Ferdinand himself only makes it as far as the Philippines, where he's killed by a tribal chief who doesn't want to listen to his Catholic talk.

Seventeenth Century

And look who we have here: a whole load of Dutchmen. Willem Barentsz is being contrary and sailing to the north. He puts Spitsbergen and Nova Zembla on the map for the Netherlands. Mind you don't get stuck in the ice, Willem. Oops, looks like it's winter with polar bears for him. Okay, then, how about Willem Janszoon? He lands in Australia, shrugs, and leaves. We're never going to complete the world map at this rate. Abel Tasman sails to New Zealand and Tasmania but gives Australia a wide berth. And here we have James Cook, stumbling into the east coast of Australia. Unlike the Dutch, the British don't seem to mind this continent, although the Aboriginals don't look too happy about things. And I can also see a slight disappointment among the fans of Terra Incognita—they really had something else in mind.

Nineteenth Century

So now we've just about got the outlines of the continents on the map. Let's bring out the landlubbers! We're still looking for the sources of the Nile, the course of the Orinoco, Lake Chad, Uluru, Kilimanjaro, Victoria Falls, the Mekong, Machu Picchu, the tops of the Himalayas, and a bunch more stuff. Off you go! Fill in the inland areas. And we're looking for enthusiasts to take a trip to the poles. I can see some candidates from Norway, the United States, England . . . Hey, don't forget your gloves, guys!

Drumroll . . .

And the winners are . . . all the countries that grew wealthy from the trade in gold, spices, slaves, rubber, and so on. But then there are so many who did not fare well in this map race: that would be pretty much all the people who were "discovered." The weapons and the diseases that the discoverers brought with them meant that there weren't too many of them left. So, guys, I hope you enjoyed the show. Thanks for watching. I'll see you next time on . . . *Guess the World Maaaap!*

KNOWING WHERE YOU ARE

Most seafarers and explorers were real daredevils. Until late into the eighteenth century, it was almost impossible to judge your position at sea correctly. And that position could mean the difference between shipwreck and the discovery of a new continent. Or between scurvy and an island full of exotic fruits and fresh water.

Missed Turn

In October 1628, the Dutch East India ship *Batavia* left the Netherlands on its way to the Dutch East Indies with a big load of silver coins, wine, cheese, and jewels. Almost six months later, it arrived in the south of Africa, at the Cape of Good Hope. After the crew had recovered a little and had taken on board food and drink, the ship traveled on. As with most ships at that time, the

helmsman chose the route with the fastest westerly winds. All they had to do to reach Indonesia was turn north at the right time. The map had a vague line indicating part of Australia, but not the islands that were just off the coast. It probably wouldn't have made much difference, though, because when the *Batavia* hit the reef by these islands at full speed, no one was thinking about the turn for the Dutch East Indies yet. The ship had simply sailed much faster than they thought, and so they had lost track of their position.[3]

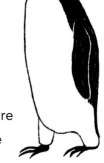

A Knotty Problem

Sailing to the west or east was a breeze. You just needed to make sure you were sailing parallel to the equator. You could work out your distance

from the equator by measuring the height of the sun in the sky. It was much more difficult, though, to calculate how far you'd already sailed to the west or east. The crew of the *Batavia* tried to estimate the distance by looking at the color of the water, the seaweed, and the birds circling above the ship. They measured the speed with a rope full of knots at regular intervals. The rope had a weighted piece of wood tied to it, which they threw overboard. Then they measured how quickly it disappeared by counting the knots. You can imagine that it wouldn't be all that accurate. For example, they didn't factor in the current of the water at all. And that's how you can bump into the reefs off the coast of Australia much sooner than you anticipated.

Crossing Lines

Imagine you want to meet someone in town. Then it's not a great idea to arrange to meet on Long Street. Long Street is pretty long; you could end up looking for each other all day. But you can make the

place perfectly clear by agreeing to meet on the corner of Long Street and another street. If you just name one street, your potential meeting spot could be miles long. If you name two streets, all you've got is the crossing point—can't miss it!

So, in order to determine your position, you need two lines that cross. That's why, on almost all maps and globes, you'll see a grid of lines. There are 180 lines running parallel to the equator (lines of latitude) and 360 lines running from pole to pole (lines of longitude). However, they're not all indicated on most maps.

The lines are numbered. The first line above the equator, for example, is 1 degree north. The first line to the east of London is 1 degree east. The wreck of the *Batavia* was found at 28.490 degrees and 113.793 degrees east. The figures after the period make the degrees as accurate as possible. If you fill in -28.490—113.793 on Google Maps—you can see on exactly which islands the survivors of the disaster spent their last days.

Important Lines

The equator divides the Earth into a northern hemisphere and a southern one. Above the equator, ninety circles are drawn; we call them the northern latitudes. Below the equator, there are also ninety circles—the southern latitudes. Every circle is a degree. The equator is at 0 degrees, and the North Pole is at 90 degrees.

There is also a line dividing the Earth into a western and an eastern hemisphere: the prime meridian, a sort of vertical equator. The prime meridian is a line from pole to pole, which runs through Greenwich, London. To the east of the prime meridian, 180 lines are drawn—the eastern longitudes. There are another 180 lines to the west of the prime meridian—the western longitudes. Every line is one degree. The prime meridian is at 0 degrees; the international dateline, on the other side of the world, is at 180 degrees. We have agreed that the day begins there.

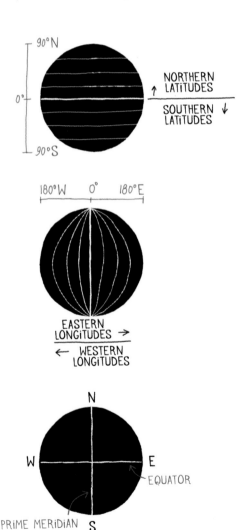

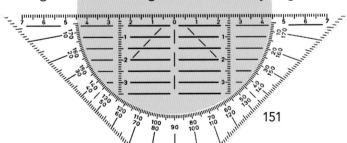

151

You Have Reached Your Destination

If you crash into a coral reef in the twenty-first century, you're doing a pretty poor job. Nowadays, any boat worthy of the name has its own radar and GPS. You probably have GPS yourself on your phone, and your parents have it in the car. It makes sure that you always know where you are. GPS is short for "global positioning system." The power of the technology actually extends a little beyond the globe, though, as it works with twenty-four satellites

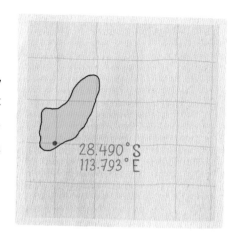

up at around 12,500 miles that orbit around the Earth in twelve hours.[4] That means that every GPS receiver on Earth is within reach of enough satellites. The system's voice knows exactly when to say what because the device is constantly calculating its distance from three satellites. It knows, for example, that you're 12,500 miles from satellite A, 12,000 miles from satellite B, and 13,000 miles from satellite C. And if you combine those three distances, there is only point on Earth where you can be.

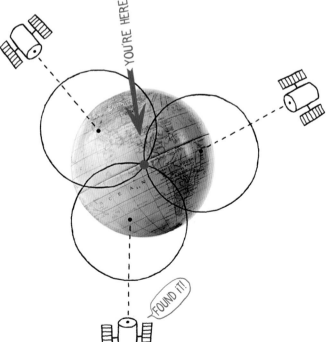

GOOGLE EARTH VIEW

• In a set of coordinates, the first number before the period shows how far north or south something is. Is there a minus sign in front of it? Then it's in the southern hemisphere.

• The second number tells you how far east or west something is. Is there a minus in front of it? Then it's in the western hemisphere.

• The coordinates 0,0 are at the point where the equator meets the prime meridian.

AROUND THE WORLD iN EiGHTY MOUSE CLiCKS

More Coordinates

Here are some fun coordinates to take a look at in Google Earth View. Google for *Earth View* in the latest version of the Chrome internet browser. Type the following coordinates into the Search function and see where you end up. Sometimes there is a *Places near* tab once you've typed in the coordinates; click on that, and you'll see information about where you traveled. (*See last page of book for answers.*)

40.821, 14.426[a]	-33.8563, 151.215[e]	32.154, -110.830[i]
29.975, 31.13[b]	-13.16, -72.54[f]	31.208, 7.861[j]
35.03, -111.02[c]	27.988, 86.925[g]	62.527, 113.993[k]
-17.923, 25.856[d]	25.226, 55.172[h]	22.25, 113.90[l]

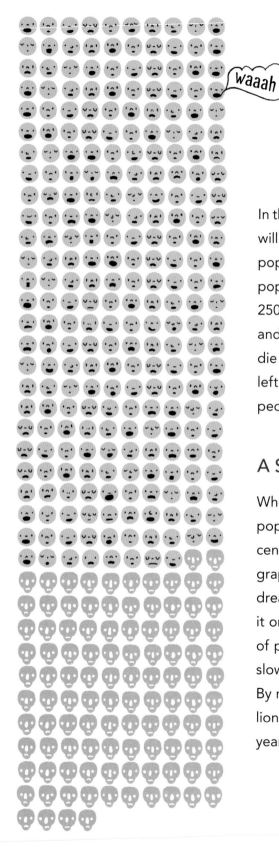

waaah

PEOPLE, PEOPLE, PEOPLE

In the time it takes you to read this sentence, twenty children will have been born into the world. Pop, pop, pop, pop, pop, pop, pop, pop, pop, pop, pop, pop, pop, pop, pop, pop, pop, pop, pop, pop. Can you picture them? Every minute, 250 new Earth dwellers come along. That's 360,000 per day and more than 131 million per year. Luckily, 55 million people die every year. Otherwise there really would be no space left in the world. But that still means an extra 76 million new people a year, more than the entire population of Thailand.[5]

A Steep Rise

When people began with agriculture 10,000 years ago, the population slowly started to grow. But it is mainly in the past century that lots of lots of new people have been born. A graph of the world's population looks like every skater's dream: steeper than the steepest halfpipe. It's just too bad it only goes up on one side. It would show that the number of people stays the same for a very long time, then it rises slowly before finally shooting straight up, almost vertically. By now we've reached a world population of over seven billion and another billion come along about every thirteen years. This is mainly because people aren't dying as young.

A Nice, Long Life

Your grandma's grandma's grandma's grandma could count herself lucky if she reached the age of forty. Nowadays most grandmas in the United States make it to seventy or eighty, and the chance is pretty high that one day you'll be older than one hundred. We have a few clever inventions and discoveries to thank for that, which were made in the past century and a half. For example, we don't poo into buckets anymore but use toilets connected to sewers. Then we wash our hands with soap.

We have antibiotics to fight bacteria that could make us sick, we are vaccinated against contagious diseases, we use fertilizer to increase the size of our harvests, and we no longer throw trash out the window or into the water but have it collected by the garbage truck. And most people drink water from a faucet instead of directly from a river. These are all developments that were unimaginable 150 years ago and that help us to live longer. Hoorah!

Major Metropolises

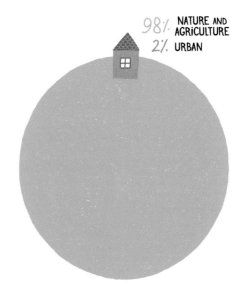

98% NATURE AND AGRICULTURE
2% URBAN

However, it isn't always that easy to find people on the globe. Use your finger to point at ten random places on the world map. If you get a wet finger, you can try again. There's a good chance that all ten of the places will have hardly any inhabitants, or even none at all. People are in the habit of sticking together. More than half the people in the world live in a town or city. And that number is quickly increasing. Machines and other inventions mean that fewer people are needed in the countryside. Besides, a lot of people think they can earn more money in the city. They might end up disappointed. For many, this move to the city means moving to substandard housing, where hundreds of thousands of poor people find themselves living in rickety or unhealthy places that are not really suitable for habitation. The biggest cities in the world are in Asia, but the cities of Africa and South America are growing quickly too. For now, Tokyo is the most populated city of all, with nearly 40 million inhabitants. New York, the only US city on the top-ten list, doesn't even have 19 million—and that's with the population of neighbor Newark, New Jersey, too.[6]

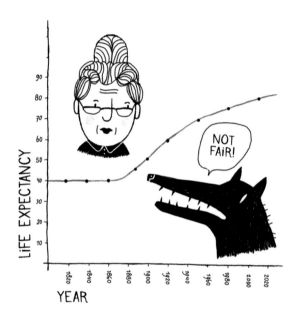

Rapid Growth

Two hundred years ago, there were not even a billion people in the whole world. There were no cities with a million inhabitants, no skyscrapers, no supermarkets. In most places, the nights were pitch-dark, as there was no electric lighting. The quickest way to get from point A to point B in places such as the United States and Europe was to travel by stagecoach. And it would take up to two days, with a night at an inn halfway, to journey one hundred twenty-five miles. There were no airplanes, no trains, no cars, and no traffic jams. And no, there were no nuclear weapons, no chemical plants, no factory farming, and no plastic bags blowing around.

Your grandma's grandma's grandma's grandma would hardly recognize the world today. And she certainly couldn't have predicted all the changes. Maybe it's even more difficult to predict what the world will be like one day when you're a grandma or a grandpa. Even

though that's not nearly as far away. All those billions of new people are simply bursting with ideas. They're going to make lots more inventions and discoveries than have happened in the past two centuries. Maybe a pill to treat flu, a campsite on Mars, a fuel with no drawbacks . . . The world will look very different in fifty years' time. And very different than you could imagine.

THE END OF THE WORLD

There will come a time when there is no Earth. But that'll be a long time yet. Our planet has been around for 4.5 billion years or so, and it'll probably continue to exist for at least as long again. But after that, it'll be gone for good. The water in the oceans will evaporate, the Earth's crust will melt, and if we're really unlucky, the whole ball of lava will be swallowed by the sun. There's no sunscreen strong enough to deal with that.

Let's Skedaddle!

We still have all the time in the world to get out of here. Ten thousand years was all it took to swap our bearskins for jeans, campfires for screens, and bare feet for high-speed trains. So a few billion years should be enough to build a new colony—in this solar system or somewhere beyond—for all those people who have to leave the Earth. There are already plans to make Mars a second home planet. And it can't be much longer before we find a planet outside our solar system where life is possible, like on

Earth. Maybe in a thousand years, or a billion years, we'll have found a way to fly there. If we're still around . . .

Some Ways to Become Extinct

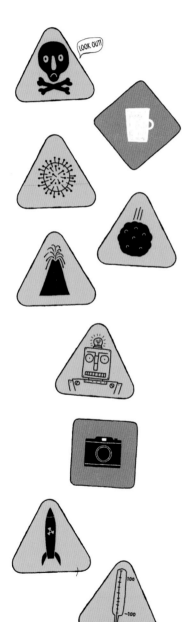

A billion years is an unimaginable length of time. A billion years ago there was barely any life on Earth, let alone fish, reptiles, birds, or mammals. The dinosaurs came along 230 million years ago and roamed the Earth for 165 million years—almost a thousand times as long as humans have been around—until a lump of rock fell to Earth and wiped out nearly all the dinosaurs. Of all the species that have ever existed on Earth, more than 90 percent have become extinct. Other animals and plants have taken their place. So why shouldn't human beings die out too?

Some people think that we're already heading toward extinction fast, and it's all our own fault. Nuclear weapons, climate change, overpopulation, robots with minds of their own, nasty viruses: they're all ways to become extinct. And the Earth itself has a few tricks up its sleeve: How about a super-volcano exploding, like at Yellowstone in the United States? It happens on average only a few times in a million years, but a supervolcano can throw so much ash into the air that it completely messes up the climate. The impact of a meteorite or a collision with a comet can also kick up a lot of dust—so much so that the sun is darkened for years, which makes the plants die, and so the plant-eaters die, and so do the meat-eaters, and so do human beings. Fortunately, scientists can see most large meteorites approaching and they're already working on a way to protect us.

The Earth's Future

We can largely predict the future of our planet. Ice ages will keep on coming and going for a while. The plates of the Earth will keep moving and constantly forming a new world map. First Africa will break in two, and Kenya will become an island in the Indian Ocean. Then Spain and Portugal will break away from Europe, and the Mediterranean Sea will close up. All of the continents will probably drift together to form a new supercontinent, surrounded by a superocean.

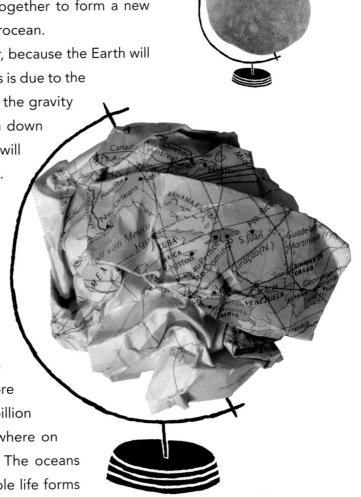

The days will last longer and longer, because the Earth will be spinning more and more slowly. This is due to the friction in the interior of the Earth and the gravity of the moon: the tides slow the Earth down a little. At the same time, the moon will keep moving farther from the Earth. That's been going on for as long as the moon has existed. It's too bad there were no eyes around to see the moon when it was ten times as large in the sky.

While the moon slowly seems to be growing smaller, the sun will shine more and more brightly. The more hydrogen the sun burns, the more light and heat it gives off. In about a billion years, the temperature almost everywhere on Earth will be well over 100 degrees. The oceans will begin to evaporate, and only simple life forms will continue to exist. In a few billion years, the hydrogen in the sun will be exhausted—finished, finito, nada—and its exterior will begin to swell. First it will swallow Mercury, then Venus. The sun will expand beyond the current orbit of the Earth, so the entire distance between our planet and the sun will be taken up by the sun.

We don't know for sure if the Earth will also be swallowed up. It's possible that the Earth will have moved by then. But in any case, the sun will be so close that the oceans will completely evaporate and the entire planet will change into a big ball of lava where all life will be impossible. Eventually, that ball will collide with the remains of our sun.

The End

Sometimes, when the sun is about to set or is hiding behind a thin cloud, you can take a quick look at it. Then you'll see a circle, just as almost every Earth dweller has drawn as a child with yellow pencils or felt-tip pens. Sometimes with a few rays, sometimes with a friendly face. Remember that the tiny little sun is more than a million times the size of the Earth, which isn't all that puny itself. So you can imagine how far away the sun is from us. And just feel how much warmth it gives us, even at this distance. Just think how hot it would be if you were close to it. Then look beneath your feet, at that ball full of glowing-hot iron and magma. Sit on the sand that the rivers have carried from the mountains. Take another deep breath of our fresh atmosphere. And enjoy lying on the Earth's crust, where billions of people and animals are walking around as they fly at an incredible speed through the universe. That is how it feels to be an Earth dweller.

THE SALT OF THE EARTH DWELLERS

I would like to thank a few people who helped me to write this book. Thanks to their critical reading and suggestions, you shouldn't have come across any nonsense in this book, all being well. Bernd Andeweg made sure that I didn't make the magma too liquid and that the glaciers left scratches in the mountains. Mark van Heck made the Earth's crust thicker and made sure that the trees didn't take too much credit for absorbing the CO_2. Coen Klein Douwel helped me mainly to dig up the truth about high tide and low tide and to fathom photosynthesis. Govert Schilling was responsible, among other things, for making sure that the spaceships on Venus weren't flattened entirely and that there was enough nitrogen in the atmosphere. Finally, Edith Schouten is the finest Earth dweller of all. She encouraged me and slowed me down, at exactly the right moments.

NOTES

Chapter 1

1. "10—Measures of the Planets," Multiverse, University of California, Berkeley Space Sciences Laboratory, accessed April 2018, http://cse.ssl.berkeley.edu/AtHomeAstronomy/act10_datasheet.html.

2. Tim Sharp, "How Big Is the Sun?/Size of the Sun," Space.com, October 31, 2017, https://www.space.com/17001-how-big-is-the-sun-size-of-the-sun.html.

3. *National Geographic*, s.v. "equator," accessed April 2018, https://www.nationalgeographic.org/encyclopedia/equator/.

4. Read more about the controversy surrounding measuring Mount Everest. Bhadra Sharma and Kai Schultz, "How Tall Is Mount Everest? For Nepal, It's a Touchy Question," *New York Times*, February 3, 2018, https://www.nytimes.com/2018/02/03/world/asia/mount-everest-how-tall-nepal.html.

5. Becky Oskin, "Mariana Trench: The Deepest Depths," *Live Science*, December 6, 2017, https://www.livescience.com/23387-mariana-trench.html.

6. "The Coldest Place in the World," NASA Science, December 10, 2013, https://science.nasa.gov/science-news/science-at-nasa/2013/09dec_coldspot/.

7. "Death Valley Weather," National Park Service, last updated January 11, 2018, https://www.nps.gov/deva/planyourvisit/weather.htm.

8. Tim Sharp, "What Is Earth's Average Temperature?" Space.com, April 23, 2018, https://www.space.com/17816-earth-temperature.html.

9. Elizabeth Howell, "How Fast Is Earth Moving?" Space.com, July 23, 2016, https://www.space.com/33527-how-fast-is-earth-moving.html.

10. "How Far Away Is the Moon?" NASA Space Place, last updated May 25, 2017, https://spaceplace.nasa.gov/moon-distance/en/.

11. "What Is Jupiter?" NASA Knows!, July 8, 2016, https://www.nasa.gov/audience/forstudents/k-4/stories/nasa-knows/what-is-jupiter-k4.html.

12. "What Is Mercury?" NASA Knows!, March 30, 2011, https://www.nasa.gov/audience/forstudents/5-8/features/nasa-knows/what-is-planet-mercury-58.html.

13. Nicholas Gerbis, "How Much Would You Weigh on Other Planets?" *Live Science*, June 24, 2011, https://www.livescience.com/33356-weight-on-planets-mars-moon.html.

14. "Missions to Venus and Mercury," The Planetary Society, accessed April 2018, http://www.planetary.org/explore/space-topics/space-missions/missions-to-venus-mercury.html.

15. "How Big Is Our Solar System?" NASA, accessed April 2018, https://www.nasa.gov/sites/default/files/files/YOSS_Act1.pdf.

16. "Solar System Temperatures," NASA, accessed April 2018, https://solarsystem.nasa.gov/resources/681/solar-system-temperatures/.

17. "Planets and Moons," European Space Agency, accessed April 2018, https://www.esa.int/esaKIDSen/SEMD88BE8JG_OurUniverse_0.html.

18. "Planets," NASA Science, accessed April 2018, https://solarsystem.nasa.gov/planets/in-depth/.

19. Jennifer Frazer, "What Lives at the Bottom of the Mariana Trench? More Than You Might Think," *Scientific American*, April 14, 2013, https://blogs.scientificamerican.com/artful-amoeba/what-lives-at-the-bottom-of-the-mariana-trench-more-than-you-might-think/.

20. "The Goldilocks Zone," NASA Science, October 2, 2003, https://science.nasa.gov/science-news/science-at-nasa/2003/02oct_goldilocks.

21. Jonathan Amos, "Dinosaur Asteroid Hit 'Worst Possible Place,'" BBC, May 15, 2017, http://www.bbc.com/news/science-environment-39922998.

22. "The Glanerbrug Meteorite Fall," Dutch Meteor Society, accessed April 2018, https://dmsweb.home.xs4all.nl/meteorites/glanerbrug/glanerbrug.html.

23. Walter Jansen, adapted by Marlene Rau and Andrew Brown, "The Dog's Cave (*Grotta del Cane*)," *Science in Schools*, 20, http://www.scienceinschool.org/sites/default/files/teaserMaterial/issue20_CO2_stories.pdf.

24. "What Is Earth?" NASA Knows!, October 4, 2017, https://www.nasa.gov/audience/forstudents/5-8/features/nasa-knows/what-is-earth-58.html.

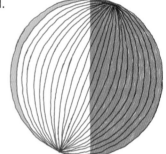

Chapter 2

1. Howell, "How Fast Is Earth Moving?"; Seth Kadish, "Tangential Speed of Earth's Surface Due to Rotational Motion," January 2014, *Vizual Statistix*, http://vizual-statistix.tumblr.com/post/74287163429/have-you-ever-wondered-how-fast-you-are-spinning.

2. Scott Neuman, "1 in 4 Americans Thinks the Sun Goes Around the Earth, Survey Says," NPR, February 14, 2014, https://www.npr.org/sections/thetwo-way/2014/02/14/277058739/1-in-4-americans-think-the-sun-goes-around-the-earth-survey-says.

3. Elizabeth Nix, "When Did the United States Start Using Time Zones?" *Scientific American*, April 8, 2015, https://www.history.com/news/ask-history/when-did-the-united-states-start-using-time-zones.

4. Rhett Herman, "How Fast Is the Earth Moving?" *Scientific American*, accessed April 2018, https://www.scientificamerican.com/article/how-fast-is-the-earth-mov/.

5. "What Causes the Seasons?" NASA Space Place, last updated October 27, 2016, https://spaceplace.nasa.gov/seasons/en/.

6. The Editors of *Encyclopaedia Britannica*, "Julian Calendar," *Encyclopaedia Britannica*, January 5, 2018, https://www.britannica.com/science/Julian-calendar.

7. The Editors of *Encyclopaedia Britannica*, "Gregorian Calendar," *Encyclopaedia Britannica*, accessed April 2018, https://www.britannica.com/topic/Gregorian-calendar.

8. "Tilt and Latitude," North Carolina Climate Office, accessed April 2018, https://climate .ncsu.edu/edu/Tilt.

Chapter 3

1. William E. Holt and Terry C. Wallace, "Crustal Thickness and Upper Mantle velocities in the Tibetan Plateau Region from the Inversion of Regional PNL Waveforms: Evidence for a Thick Upper Mantle Lid Beneath Southern Tibet," *Journal of Geophysical Research*, 95 (August 1990): B8, 12499–12525, doi: 10.1029/JB095iB08p12499.

2. "Earth's Interior," *National Geographic*, accessed April 2018. https://www .nationalgeographic.com/science/earth/surface-of-the-earth/earths-interior/.

3. "The Earth's Layers Lesson #1," Volcano World, Oregon State University, accessed April 2018, http://volcano.oregonstate.edu/earths-layers-lesson-1.

4. "Beneath Earth's Surface, Scientists Find Long 'Fingers' of Heat," *Science Daily*, September 5, 2013, https://www.sciencedaily.com/releases/2013/09/130905142815.htm.

5. Natalie Angier, "The Enigma 1,800 Miles Below Us," *New York Times*, May 28, 2012, https://www.nytimes.com/2012/05/29/science/earths-core-the-enigma-1800-miles -below-us.html.

6. Alicia Ault, "Ask Smithsonian: What's the Deepest Hole Ever Dug?" *Smithsonian.com*, February 19, 2015, https://www.smithsonianmag.com/smithsonian-institution/ask -smithsonian-whats-deepest-hole-ever-dug-180954349/.

7. *National Geographic*, s.v. "continental drift," accessed April 2018, https://www .nationalgeographic.org/encyclopedia/continental-drift/.

8. The Editors of *Encyclopaedia Britannica*, "Alfred Wegener," *Encyclopaedia Britannica*, February 23, 2017, https://www.britannica.com/biography/Alfred-Wegener.

9. NOAA, "What Is the Longest Mountain Range on Earth?" National Oceanic and Atmospheric Adminstration, last updated October 10, 2017, https://oceanservice.noaa .gov/facts/midoceanridge.html.

10. Charles Q. Choi, "Fossils Found in Alps Suggest Deep Sea Played Key Role in Evolution of Marine Life," *Huffington Post*, May 22, 2014, https://www.huffingtonpost.com/2014/ 05/22 /deep-sea-fossils-evolution_n_5371906.html.

11. Adam Voiland, "The Eight-Thousanders," NASA Earth Observatory, December 16, 2013, https://earthobservatory.nasa.gov/Features/8000MeterPeaks/.

12. "Fossils Found in Tibet Revise History of Elevation, Climate," *Science Daily*, June 12, 2008, https://www.sciencedaily.com/releases/2008/06/080611144021.htm.

13. Jennifer Chu, "India Drift," MIT News Office, May 4, 2015, http://news.mit.edu/2015/india -drift-eurasia-0504.

14. "The Himalayas: Two Continents Collide," US Geological Survey, last updated September 3, 2015, https://pubs.usgs.gov/gip/dynamic/himalaya.html.

15. David Bressan, "October 23, 4004 B.C.: Happy Birthday Earth!" *Scientific American*, October 22, 2013, https://blogs.scientificamerican.com/history-of-geology/october-23 -4004-bc-happy-birthday-earth/.

16. The Editors of *Encyclopaedia Britannica*, "Peru-Chile Trench," *Encyclopaedia Britannica*, July 20, 1998, https://www.britannica.com/place /Peru-Chile-Trench.

17. *National Geographic*, s.v. "Ring of Fire," accessed April 2018, https://www .nationalgeographic.org/encyclopedia/ring -fire/.

18. "Amateur Trail Runner Makes History on South America's Highest Peak," *National Geographic*, February 9, 2018, https://www .nationalgeographic.com/adventure/features/athletes/trail-runner-first-woman-complete-full -360-route-aconcagua-argentina/.

19. "Denali or Mount McKinley?" National Park Service, 2015, https://www.nps.gov/dena /learn/historyculture/denali-origins.htm.

20. Tribune Wire Reports, "North America's Tallest Mountain Gets New Name—And Height," *Chicago Tribune*, September 2, 2015, http://www.chicagotribune.com /news/nationworld/ct-denali-height-20150902-story.html.

21. Henry Stedman, "What Is the Height of Kilimanjaro?" Climb Mount Kilimanjaro, accessed April 2018, https://www.climbmountkilimanjaro.com/.

22. The Editors of *Encyclopaedia Britannica*, "Mount Elbrus," *Encyclopaedia Britannica*, June 2, 2017, https://www.britannica.com/place/Mount-Elbrus.

23. Kim Ann Zimmerman, "Mount Vinson: Antarctica's Highest Mountain," Live Science, November 11, 2013, https://www.livescience.com/41122-mount-vinson-antarcticas-highest -mountain.html.

24. The Editors of *Encyclopaedia Britannica*, "Jaya Peak," *Encyclopaedia Britannica*, November 17, 2017, https://www.britannica.com/place/Jaya-Peak.

25. The Editors of *Encyclopaedia Britannica*, "Mount Blanc," *Encyclopaedia Britannica*, April 30, 2013, https://www.britannica.com/place/Mont-Blanc-mountain-Europe.

26. Jennifer Nalewicki, "Seven Surprising Facts About the Matterhorn," Smithsonian.com, March 9, 2016, https://www.smithsonianmag.com/travel/seven-surprising-facts-about -matterhorn-180958192/.

27. The Editors of *Encyclopaedia Britannica*, "Mount Etna," *Encyclopaedia Britannica*, April 20, 2018, https://www.britannica.com/place/Mount-Etna.

28. "About Uluru and Kata Tjuta," Parks Australia, accessed April 2018, https://parksaustralia .gov.au/uluru/people-place/amazing-facts.html.

29. The Editors of *Encyclopaedia Britannica*, "Asthenosphere," *Encyclopaedia Britannica*, April 1, 2015, https://www.britannica.com/science/asthenosphere.

30. History.com Staff, "Krakatoa Erupts," History.com, 2009, https://www.history.com/this-day -in-history/krakatoa-erupts.

31. Simon Winchester, *Krakatoa: The Day the World Exploded*: August 27, 1883 (New York: Harper Perennial, 2005).

32. "Anak Krakatau," Atlas Obscura, accessed April 2018, https://www .atlasobscura.com/places/anak-krakatau.

33. History.com Staff, "Pompeii," History.com, 2010, accessed June 2018, https://www.history.com/topics/ancient-history/pompeii.

34. Nanna Gunnarsdóttir, "Volcanoes in Iceland," Guide to Iceland, accessed April 2018, https://guidetoiceland.is/nature-info/the -deadliest-volcanoes-in-iceland.

35. "Temperatures at the Surface Reflect Temperatures Below the Ground," US Geological Survey, accessed April 2018, https://volcanoes.usgs.gov/vhp/thermal.html.

36. "Eyjafjallajökull Eruption, Iceland April/May 2010," British Geological Survey, accessed April 2018, http://www.bgs.ac.uk/research/volcanoes/icelandic_ash.html.

37. "Landslides Are Common on Tall, Steep, and Weak Volcanic Cones," US Geological Survey, accessed April 2018, https://volcanoes.usgs.gov/vhp/landslides.html.

38. Walter Sullivan, "Studies Find Warnings of Volcano Were in Vain," *The New York Times: Archives*, June 29, 1986, accessed June 2018, https://www.nytimes.com/1986/06/29/us /studies-find-warnings-of-volcano-were-in-vain.html.

39. "Chaine des Puys, France," Volcano World, Oregon State University, accessed April 2018, http://volcano.oregonstate.edu/vwdocs/volc_images/europe_west_asia/france/puys.html.

40. "West Eifel Volcanic Field," Smithsonian Institution, National Museum of Natural History, Global Volcanism Program, accessed April 2018, https://volcano.si.edu/volcano .cfm?vn=210010.

41. "Zuidwal volcano," Wikipedia, accessed June 2018, https://en.wikipedia.org/wiki/Zuidwal _volcano.

42. "2011 Japan Earthquake-Tsunami Fast Facts," CNN, last updated March 16, 2018, https:// www.cnn.com/2013/07/17/world/asia/japan-earthquake---tsunami-fast-facts/index.html.

43. "Earthquake Facts," US Geological Survey, accessed April 2018, https://earthquake.usgs .gov/learn/facts.php.

44. "How Often Do Earthquakes Occur?", Education and Outreach Series No. 3, IRIS: Incorporated Research Institutions for Seismology, accessed June 2018, https://www.iris .edu/hq/inclass/fact-sheet/how_often_do_earthquakes_occur.

45. "Did You Feel It? Oklahoma Rattled by Early Morning Earthquake," KFOR, February 25, 2016, http://kfor.com/2016/02/25/did-you-feel-it-oklahoma-rattled-by-early-morning -earthquake/.

46. "Factbox: Japan's Many Earthquakes," Reuters World News, July 16, 2007, https:// www.reuters.com/article/us-quake-japan-factbox/factbox-japans-many-earthquakes -idUST32929520070717.

47. Jesselyn Cook, "7 Years After Haiti's Earthquake, Millions Still Need Aid," *Huffington Post*, January 12, 2017, https://www.huffingtonpost.com/entry/haiti-earthquake-anniversary _us_5875108de4b02b5f858b3f9c.

48. "The Tsunami Heights Observed at 2011 Tohoku Earthquake," Wikipedia, accessed June 2018, https://en.wikipedia.org/wiki/2011_Tōhoku_earthquake_and_tsunami#/media /File:Tsunami_map_Tohoku2011.svg.

49. Ed Yong, "Japanese Animals Are Still Washing Up in America After the Tsunami," *The Atlantic*, September 28 2017, https://www.theatlantic.com/science/archive/2017/09 /japanese-animals-are-still-washing-up-in-america-after-the-2011-tsunami/541347/.

Chapter 4

1. "Water's Family Tree: Where Did It Come From?" NASA's Global Precipitation Measurement mission, accessed April 2018, https://pmm.nasa.gov/education /sites/default/files/lesson_plan_files/Waters%20Family%20Tree.pdf.

2. "Glacier Landforms: Erratics," National Park Service, accessed April 2018, https://www.nps.gov/articles/erratics.htm; NPS/Diane Renkin, "Glaciers," National Park Service, last updated August 12, 2016, https:// www.nps.gov/yell/learn/nature/glaciers.htm.

3. "The Activities in the Hautes Fagnes Region in the Ardennes," Domaine des Haute Fagnes, accessed April 2018, http://www.dhf.be/en/pages/activites-dans-la-region.aspx.

4. Lewis Owen, Aleksey Nilovich Kosarev et al., "Caspian Sea," *Encyclopaedia Britannica*, November 10, 2017, https://www.britannica.com/place/Caspian-Sea.

5. The Editors of *Encyclopaedia Britannica*, "Lake Superior," *Encyclopaedia Britannica*, January 8, 2018, https://www.britannica.com/place/Lake-Superior-lake-North-America.

6. Grigory Ivanovich Galazy, "Lake Baikal," *Encyclopaedia Britannica*, April 13, 2018, https://www.britannica.com/place/Lake-Baikal.

7. The Editors of *Encyclopaedia Britannica*, "Lake Victoria," *Encyclopaedia Britannica*, November 10, 2016, https://www.britannica.com/place/Lake-Victoria.

8. The Editors of *Encyclopaedia Britannica*, "Lake Titicaca," *Encyclopaedia Britannica*, May 10, 2017, https://www.britannica.com/place/Lake-Titicaca.

9. Kenneth Pletcher, "Dead Sea," *Encyclopaedia Britannica*, January 5, 2018, https://www.britannica.com/place/Dead-Sea.

10. "*Interesting Facts About Loch Ness*, Nature: Just Fun Facts," accessed June 2018, http://justfunfacts.com/interesting-facts-about-loch-ness/.

11. Lea Monroe, "There's an Abandoned Mine Hiding in New York and It'll Absolutely Fascinate You," Only in Your State, January 28, 2017, http://www.onlyinyourstate.com/new-york/widow-jane-mine-ny/.

12. "Son Doong Cave—Overview," SonDoongCave.org, accessed April 2018, http://www.sondoongcave.org/son-doong-cave-overview.html.

13. Máté Petrány, "Ever Wondered How Much Copper Goes into Electric Cars?" *Jalopnik*, March 19, 2015, https://jalopnik.com/ever-wondered-how-much-copper-goes-into-electric-cars-1692424366.

14. "When Did Dinosaurs Live?" Natural History Museum, accessed April 2018, http://www.nhm.ac.uk/discover/dino-directory/about-dinosaurs/when-did-dinosaurs-live.html.

Chapter 5

1. William Langewiesche, "The Man Who Pierced the Sky," *Vanity Fair*, May 2013, https://www.vanityfair.com/culture/2013/05/felix-baumgartner-jump-story; "The Atmosphere," RedBull Stratos, accessed June 2018, http://www.redbullstratos.com/science/the-atmosphere/index.html.

2. "Meteorology: Vertical Temperature Profile of the Atmosphere," Central Weather Bureau, accessed May 2018, https://www.cwb.gov.tw/V7e/knowledge/encyclopedia/me006.htm.

3. "Earth's Atmosphere: Composition, Climate & Weather," Space.com, accessed May 2018, https://www.space.com/17683-earth-atmosphere.html.

4. "The Troposphere," Physics Department, University of California Santa Barbara, accessed April 2018, https://web.physics.ucsb.edu/~lgrace/chem123/troposphere.htm.

5. "Merida's Cable Car," Venezuelatuya, accessed April 2018, https://www.venezuelatuya.com/andes/telefericoeng.htm.

6. The Ocean Portal Team, "Sea Level Rise," Smithsonian National Museum of History, accessed April 2018, http://ocean.si.edu/sea-level-rise.

7. "Why an Ice Age Occurs Every 100,000 Years: Climate and Feedback Effects Explained," *Science Daily*, August 7, 2013, https://www.sciencedaily.com/releases/2013/08/130807134127.htm.

8. "Milankovitch Cycles and Glaciation," Indiana University, accessed April 2018, http://www.indiana.edu/~geol105/images/gaia_chapter_4/milankovitch.htm.

9. Jennifer Gray, "Higher Seas to Flood Dozens of US Cities, Study Says; Is Yours One of Them?" CNN, July 31, 2017, https://www.cnn.com/2017/07/12/us/weather-cities-inundated-climate-change/index.html.

10. Qiancheng Ma, "Greenhouse Gases: Refining the Role of Carbon Dioxide," NASA's Goddard Institute for Space Studies, March 1998, https://www.giss.nasa.gov/research/briefs/ma_01/.

11. "Climate Change Indicators: Greenhouse Gases," United States Environmental Protection Agency, accessed April 2018, https://www.epa.gov/climate-indicators/greenhouse-gases.

12. "How is Today's Warming Different from the Past?", NASA Earth Observatory, accessed June 2018, https://earthobservatory.nasa.gov/Features/GlobalWarming/page3 .php?src=share; Michon Scott, "What's the Hottest Earth has Been 'Lately'?", NOAA: Climate.gov, September 17, 2014, https://www.climate.gov/news-features/climate-qa /what's-hottest-earth-has-been-"lately"; Michael McCarthy, "Here Is the Weather for the Next Century," Independent, October 16, 1998, https://www.independent.co.uk/news /here-is-the-weather-for-next-century-1178656.html.

13. Amy Lieberman, "Preparing for the Inevitable Sea-Level Rise," The Atlantic, February 29, 2016, https://www .theatlantic.com/science/archive/2016/02/rising-sea -levels/471417/.

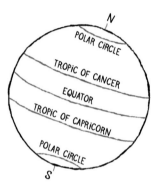

14. Tatiana Schlossberg, "Flying Is Bad for the Planet. You Can Help Make It Better," New York Times, July 27, 2017, https:// www.nytimes.com/2017/07/27/climate/airplane-pollution -global-warming.html.

15. Jacob Silverman, "Do Cows Pollute as Much As Cars?," How Stuff Works.com, accessed May 2018, https://animals.howstuffworks.com/mammals/methane-cow.htm.

16. Merrit Kenndy, "Harvey, the 'Most Significant Tropical Cyclone Rainfall Even in U.S. History,'" The Two-Way: NPR, January 25, 2018, https://www.npr.org/sections/thetwo -way/2018/01/25/580689546/harvey-the-most-significant-tropical-cyclone-rainfall-event-in -u-s-history; Average Annual Precipitation by State, Current Results: Weather and Science Facts, accessed May 2018, https://www.currentresults.com/Weather/US/average-annual -state-precipitation.php.

17. "Severe Weather 101: Frequently Asked Questions About Tornados," National Severe Storms Laboratory, accessed April 2018, https://www.nssl.noaa.gov/education/svrwx101 /tornadoes/faq/.

18. Tribune News Services, "Venezuela Death Toll Estimated at 30,000," Chicago Tribune,

December 22, 1999, http://articles.chicagotribune.com/1999-12-22
/news/9912220106_1_vargas-state-president-hugo-chavez-disaster.

19. "Learn More About Wildfires," *National Geographic*, accessed April 2018,
https://www.nationalgeographic.com/environment/natural-disasters/wildfires/.

20. "What is El Niño?" Pacific Marine Environmental Laboratory, accessed April 2018,
https://www.pmel.noaa.gov/elnino/what-is-el-nino.

Chapter 6

1. Carolyn Y. Johnson, "Native Americans Migrated to the New World in Three Waves,
Harvard-led DNA Analysis Shows," Boston Globe.com, July 11, 2012, https://www.boston
.com/uncategorized/noprimarytagmatch/2012/07/11/native-americans-migrated-to-the
-new-world-in-three-waves-harvard-led-dna-analysis-shows.

2. Amber Pariona, "Worldwide Population Throughout Human History, World Atlas, April 25,
2017, https://www.worldatlas.com/articles/worldwide-population-throughout-human
-history.html.

3. Mike Dash, *Batavia's Graveyard: The True Story of the Mad Heretic Who Led History's
Bloodiest Mutiny* (New York: Three Rivers Press, 2002).

4. "GNSS Frequently Asked Questions—GPS," Federal Aviation Administration, accessed
April 2018, https://www.faa.gov/about/office_org/headquarters_offices/ato/service_units
/techops/navservices/gnss/faq/gps/#9.

5. Lucy Lamble, "With 250 Babies Born Each Minute, How Many People Can the
Earth Sustain?" *The Guardian*, April 23, 2018, https://www.theguardian.com/global
-development/2018/apr/23/population-how-many-people-can-the-earth
-sustain-lucy-lamble.

6. "Here Are 10 of the Most Populated Cities in the World," *The Jakarta Post*,
November 4, 2017, http://www.thejakartapost.com/life/2017/11/03/here-are
-10-of-the-most-populated-cities-in-the-world.html.

Marc ter Horst is a Dutch writer of nonfiction children's books. Growing up upstairs from his parents' bicycle shop he read many books and comics.

Marc studied literature, but soon found himself more interested in geology, astronomy, and evolution. Working at the National Institute for Curriculum Development he discovered his real talent was explaining complex topics in few words. He has published five books in the Netherlands, each having numerous foreign editions released throughout the world. Marc is currently working on a children's book about climate change. He lives in Nijmegen in the Netherlands with his girlfriend, two kids, and two naughty rabbits.

Wendy Panders studied graphic design at the Willem de Kooning Academy in Rotterdam. She works as an illustrator and graphic designer for magazines and papers and has illustrated many children's books.

Answers for Around the World in Eighty Mouse Clicks from page 153.

(a) Vesuvius; (b) Pyramids; (c) meteor crater; (d) Victoria Falls; (e) Sydney Opera House; (f) Machu Picchu; (g) Everest; (h) Glacier National Park; (i) Pima Air & Space Museum; (j) Sahara Desert; (k) Mir underground diamond mine; (l) Tian Tan Buddha